Speak Forth with the Original Voice

*"To Him who rides upon
the highest heavens,
which are from ancient times;
behold,
He speaks forth with His voice,
a mighty voice."*

(Psalm 68:33)

Speak Forth with the Original Voice

Dr. Jaerock Lee

Speak Forth with the Original Voice by Dr. Jaerock Lee
Published by Urim Books (Representative: Kyungtae Noh)
73, Yeouidaebang-ro 22-gil, Dongjak-gu, Seoul, Korea
www.urimbooks.com

All rights reserved. This book or parts thereof may not be reproduced in any form, stored in a retrieval system, or transmitted in any form or by any means, electronic, mechanical, photocopying, recording or otherwise, without prior written permission of the publisher.

Unless otherwise noted, all Scripture quotations are taken from the Holy Bible, NEW AMERICAN STANDARD BIBLE, ®, Copyright © 1960, 1962, 1963, 1968, 1971, 1972, 1973, 1975, 1977, 1995 by The Lockman Foundation. Used by permission.

Copyright © 2015 by Dr. Jaerock Lee
ISBN: 979-11-263-0015-0 03230
Translation Copyright © 2013 by Dr. Esther K. Chung. Used by permission.

First Published in November 2015

Previously published in Korean in 2005 by Urim Books in Seoul, Korea

Edited by Dr. Geumsun Vin
Designed by Design Team of Urim Books
Printed by Prione Printing
For more information contact: urimbook@hotmail.com

A Message on Publication

With hopes that the readers will receive answers and blessings through the original voice, which is full of the works of creation...

There are many kinds of sounds in this world. There are the beautiful chirping of the birds, innocent laughter of babies, cheering of a crowd, sound of gasoline engines, and sound of music. These are sounds that are within the audible frequency range, and there are also other sounds like ultrasound that humans cannot hear.

If the frequency of the sound is too high or too low, we cannot hear it although it actually exists. Furthermore, there are sounds that we can hear only with our heart. It is something like the voice of our conscience. And what would be the most beautiful and most powerful sound? It is the 'Original Voice' which is spoken forth by God the Creator, who is the origin of everything.

> "To Him who rides upon the highest heavens, which are from ancient times; Behold, He speaks forth with His voice, a mighty voice" (Psalm 68:33).

> "...and behold, the glory of the God of Israel was coming from the way of the east. And His voice was like the sound of many waters; and the earth shone with His glory" (Ezekiel 43:2).

In the beginning, God covered the whole universe as the Light that contained grand voice within (1 John 1:5). Then, He planned 'human cultivation' to gain true children with whom He could share true love, and He came to exist as the Triune God, as the Father, the Son, and the Holy Spirit. The original voice was contained in the Son and the Holy Spirit as it was in the Father.

When the time came, God the Trinity spoke forth with the original voice to create the heavens and the earth and all things in them. He said, *"Let there be light," "Let the waters below the heavens be gathered into one place, and let the dry land appear" "Let the earth sprout vegetation, plants yielding seed, and fruit trees on the earth bearing fruit after their kind with seed in them," "Let there be lights in the expanse of the heavens to separate the day from the night," "Let the waters teem with swarms of living creatures, and let birds fly above the earth in the open expanse of the heavens"* (Genesis 1:3; 1:9; 1:11; 1:14; 1:20).

Therefore, all created things can hear the original voice spoken forth by God the Trinity, and they obey it transcending space and time. In the Four Gospels, even non-living things, wind and waves calmed down when Jesus spoke forth with the original voice (Luke 8:24-25). When He said to a paralytic, *"Your sins are forgiven"* and *"Get up, pick up your bed and go home"* (Matthew 9:6), he got up and went back home. Those who watched this scene were awestruck and glorified God who had given such authority to men.

John 14:12 says, *"Truly, truly, I say to you, he who believes in Me, the works that I do, he will do also; and greater works than these he will do; because I go to the Father."* Now, how can we experience the works of the original voice today? We can read in the book of Acts that people were used as God's instruments to manifest God's power, to the extent that they cast away evil from their heart to cultivate holiness in them.

Peter said to a man who had not been able to walk since his birth to walk in the name of Jesus Christ the Nazarene and held his hand. Then the man stood up, and walked and leaped. When

He said to Tabitha, who was dead, "Arise," she was revived. The apostle Paul revived a dead young man called Eutychus, and when handkerchiefs or aprons were carried from his body to the sick, the diseases left them and the evil spirits went out.

This work *Speak Forth with the Original Voice* is the last book of the series 'Holiness and Power'. It shows you the way to experience the power of God through the original voice. There are also introduction of the actual works of God's power so the readers can apply the principle in their everyday lives. There are also 'Examples of the Bible' which will help the readers understand the spiritual realm and the principles in receiving the answers.

I give thanks to Geumsun Vin the director of Editorial Bureau and the staff, and I pray in the name of the Lord that as many people as possible will receive answers to prayers and blessings by experiencing the original voice that manifests the works of creation.

Jaerock Lee

Foreword

Along with the growth of the church, God let us hold "Two-Week Continuous Special Revival Meetings" from 1993 to 2004. It was for God to let the church members have spiritual faith and catch a glimpse of the dimension of goodness, light, love, and power of God. As the years passed, God let them experience in their lives the power of creation that is beyond space and time.

The messages preached in those revival meetings were compiled as 'Holiness and Power' series. *Speak Forth with the Original Voice* tells us about some of the deep spiritual things that have not been made known widely, such as: the origin of God; the original heavens; the works of power that are manifested through the original voice and how to experience them in actual lives.

Chapter 1, 'Origin' explains about who God is, how He existed, and how and why He created human beings. Chapter 2 'Heavens' explains the fact that there are many heavens and that God governs over all these heavens. It continues to assert that we can receive answers to any problem if we just believe in this God, through the example of Naaman, an army general of Aram. Chapter 3, 'Triune God' talks about why the original God divided the spaces and came to exist as the Triune God, and what each of the Trinity's roles is.

Chapter 4, 'Justice' discusses the justice of God and how we can receive the answers in accordance with that justice. Chapter 5, 'Obedience' tells us about Jesus who obeyed God's words completely, and argues that we also must obey God's words to experience God's works. Chapter 6, 'Faith' exposits that although all believers say they believe, there are differences in the degree of the answers received, and it also teaches us what we have to do to show the kind of faith that can earn the complete trust of God.

Chapter 7, 'Who do you say I am?' speaks about the way for us to receive answers with the example of Peter, who received the promise of blessing when he professed Jesus was the Lord from the depth of his heart. Chapter 8 'What do you want Me to do for you?' explains step by step the process of a blind man receiving his answer. Chapter 9 'It shall be done for you as you have believed' shows the secret for the centurion to receive his answer, and introduces the real life cases of our church.

Through this book, I pray in the name of the Lord that all the readers will understand the origin of God and the works of God the Trinity, and receive everything they ask for through their obedience and faith that is in accordance with justice, so that they can give glory to God.

April, 2009
Geumsun Vin,
Director of Editorial Bureau

Table of Contents

A Message on Publication

Foreword

Chapter 1	Origin	· 1
Chapter 2	Heavens	· 17
Chapter 3	Triune God	· 35

Examples of the Bible I

Events that took place when the gate of the second heaven opened in the first heaven

Chapter 4	Justice	· 55
Chapter 5	Obedience	· 73
Chapter 6	Faith	· 91

Examples of the Bible II
The third heaven and the space of the third dimension

Chapter 7	Who do you say I am?	· 109
Chapter 8	What do you want Me to do for you?	· 125
Chapter 9	It shall be done for you as you have believed	· 141

Examples of the Bible III
The power of God, who possesses the fourth heaven

Chapter 1 Origin

> If we understand the origin of God
> and how the human kind came to exist,
> we can do the whole duty of men.

The origin of God

The original God planned human cultivation

The image of God the Trinity

God created men to gain true children

The origin of men

The seeds of life and conception

The almighty God the Creator

*"In the beginning was the Word,
and the Word was with God,
and the Word was God."*

John 1:1

Today, many people seek meaningless things because they don't know about the origin of the universe or the true God who reigns over it. They just do whatever they please because they don't understand why they are living on this earth – the true purpose and value of life. After all, they live lives that are swaying like grass because they don't know about their origin.

However, we can believe in God and live a life doing the 'whole duty' of man if we understand the origin of God the Trinity and how men came to exist. Now, what is the origin of the Triune God, the Father, the Son, and the Holy Spirit?

The origin of God

John 1:1 tells us about God in the beginning, namely the origin of God. When is the 'beginning' here? It was before the eternity, when there was no one else but the Creator God in all the spaces of the universe. All the spaces of the universe don't indicate only the visible universe. Other than the space in the universe in which we are living, unimaginably spacious and measureless spaces exist as well. In the entire universe including all these spaces, God the Creator alone existed since before eternity.

Because everything on this earth has limits and the beginning and the end, most people cannot easily understand the concept of 'before the eternity'. Now, perhaps God could have said, "In the beginning was God," but why did He say, "In the beginning was the Word"? It's because back then God did not have the 'shape' or 'appearance' that He has now.

People of this world have limits, so they always want some kind of substantial form or shape for them to be able to see and touch. That is why they make various idols to worship. But how can man-made idols become the god who created heavens and earth and all things in them? How can they become the god who has control over life, death, fortune, and misfortune, and even human history?

God existed as the Word in the beginning, but because men would have to be able to recognize the existence of God, He put on a shape. So, how did God, who was the Word in the beginning, exist? He existed as the beautiful lights and magnificent voice. He didn't need a name or a shape. He existed as the Light that harbors the voice and governed all the spaces in the universe. As John 1:5 says that God is Light, He covered all the spaces in the entire universe with Light and harbored voice in it, and that voice is the 'Word' mentioned in John 1:1.

The original God planned human cultivation

When the time came, God who had existed as the Word in the beginning made a plan. It was 'human cultivation'. Simply stated, it is a plan to create men and let them increase in number, so that some of them would come forth as true children of God who resemble Him. Then God would take them into the kingdom of heaven and live happily forever sharing love with them.

After having this plan in His mind, God put His plan into action one step at a time. First, He divided the entire universe. I will explain about the space in more detail in the second chapter. Actually, all the spaces were just one space, and God divided the one entire space into many spaces according to the necessity of human cultivation. And a very important event took place after the division of the spaces.

Before the beginning there existed the One God, but God came to exist as the Trinity of the Father, the Son, and the Holy Spirit. It was like God the Father gave birth to God the Son and God the Holy Spirit. For this reason, the Bible refers to Jesus as the only begotten Son of God. And Hebrews 5:5 *"You are My Son, today I have begotten You."*

God the Son and God the Holy Spirit have the same heart and power because they came from the One God. The Trinity is the same in everything. For this reason Philippians 2:6-7 says about Jesus, *"...who, although He existed in the form of God, did not regard equality with God a thing to be grasped, but emptied Himself, taking the form of a bond-servant, and being made in the likeness of men."*

The image of God the Trinity

In the beginning, God existed as the Word which was harbored in the Light, but He came to have the form of God the Trinity for the sake of human cultivation. We can imagine the image of God if we think about the scene where God created man. Genesis 1:26 says, *"Let Us make man in Our image, according to Our likeness; and let them rule over the fish of the sea and over the birds of the sky and over the cattle and over all the earth, and over every creeping thing that creeps on the earth."* Here, 'Us' refers to the Trinity of the Father, the Son, and the Holy Spirit, and we can understand that we were created in the image of God the Trinity.

It says, *"Let Us make man in Our image, according to Our likeness,"* and we can also understand what kind of image God the Trinity has. Of course, creating men in the image of God does not only mean our outward appearances look like God. Man was created in the image of God inside, too; he was filled with goodness and truth inside.

But the first man Adam sinned in disobedience, and then he lost the first image given when he was created. And he corrupted and became stained with sins and evil. So, if we really understand that our body and heart were created in the image of God, we should recover this lost image of God.

God created men to gain true children

After the division of the spaces, God the Trinity began to create the necessary things one by one. For example, He did not need His dwelling place when He existed as Light and Voice. But after He put on a shape, He needed a dwelling place as well as angels and heavenly hosts serving Him. So He first created spiritual beings in the spiritual realm, and then He created all the things in the universe in which we are living.

Of course He did not create the heavens and the earth in our space just after He created everything in the spiritual realm. After God the Trinity created the spiritual realm, He had lived with the heavenly host and angels there for a boundlessly long period. After such a long period, He created all things in this physical space. And only after creating all the environments in which human beings could live did He create man in His own image.

Now what is the reason why God created man even though there were numerous angels and heavenly hosts serving Him? It's because He wanted to gain true children. True children are those who resemble God and who can share true love with God. Except for few special ones, heavenly host and angels unconditionally obey and serve, in a sense, like robots. If you think about parents and children, no parents would love obedient robots more than their own children. They love their children because they can share love with each other willingly.

Human beings on the other hand are capable of obeying and loving God with their freewill. Of course, men cannot just understand the heart of God and share love with Him as soon as they are born. They have to experience many things as they grow up, so that they can feel the love of God and realize the whole duty of men. Only these people can love God with their heart and obey His will.

Such people do not love God because they are forced to do so. They do not obey the words of God out of fear of retribution. They just love God and give thanks to Him with their own freewill. And, an attitude such as this does not change. God planned human cultivation to gain true children with whom He could share love, giving and receiving from the heart. For this to happen, He created the first man Adam.

The origin of men

Now, what is the origin of men? Genesis 2:7 says, *"Then the LORD God formed man of dust from the ground, and breathed into his nostrils the breath of life; and man became a living being."* So, men are special beings that transcend all things that the Darwinian evolutionism professes. Human beings did not evolve from the lower animals and come up to today's level. Men were created in the image of God, and God breathed the breath of life into them. This means both spirit and body came from God.

Therefore, men are spiritual beings that came from above. We should not just think of ourselves as a little bit more advanced animals than other animals. If we look into the fossils that are presented as the evidence of evolution, there are no intermediary fossils that can connect different species. On the other hand however, there is much more evidence of creation.

For example, all mankind have two eyes, two ears, one nose, and one mouth. And they are located at the same place. And. it's not just mankind. All kinds of animals also have almost the same structure. This is the evidence that all living creatures were designed by one Creator. Other than this, the fact that all things in the universe are running in a perfect order, without a single error, is the evidence of God's creation.

Today, many people think human beings evolved from animals, and thus they don't realize where they came from and why they are living here. But once we realize that we are holy beings that were created in the image of God, we can understand who our Father is. Then, we will naturally try to live by His Word and resemble Him.

We may think our father is our physical father. But if we keep on going up, the first physical father is the first man Adam. So, we can understand that our true Father is God who created human beings. Originally, the seeds of life were also given by God. In this sense, our parents just lent their bodies as instruments for those seeds to be combined and we could be conceived.

The seeds of life and conception

God gave the seed of life. He gave sperm to men and ovum to women so they could give birth to children. In this regard, men cannot give birth to children with their own ability. God gave them the seeds of life so they could give birth.

The seeds of life contain the power of God that can make

all the organs of men. They are too small to be visible to naked eye, but the personalities, appearances, habits, and the life-force are gathered in them. So, when children are born, they take after not just appearances but also the personalities of their parents.

If men have the ability to give birth, why would there be infertile couples who struggle to have babies? Conception solely belongs to God. Today, they do artificial insemination in clinics, but they can never create the sperm and ovum. The power of creation strictly belongs to God.

Many believers, not just in our church but also in other countries, experienced this power of creation of God. There were many couples that couldn't have a baby for a long time in their marriage, even as long as 20 years. They tried all the methods available but with no results. But upon receiving the prayer, many of them gave birth to healthy children.

Several years ago, a couple living in Japan attended a revival meeting here and received my prayer. They were not only healed of their sicknesses, but they also received the blessing of conception. Such news spread and many more people from Japan came to receive my prayer. They too received the blessing of conception according to their faith. This eventually led to a branch church being established in that region.

The almighty God the Creator

Today, we see the development of sophisticated medical science, but creating life can only be possible by the power of God, the governor of all life. Through His power, those who breathed their last were brought back to life; those who received death sentence from the hospital were healed; many incurable diseases that science or medicine of man cannot cure were healed.

The original voice spoken forth by God can create something out of nothing. It can manifest the works of power for which nothing is impossible. Romans 1:20 says, *"For since the creation of the world His invisible attributes, His eternal power and divine nature, have been clearly seen, being understood through what has been made, so that they are without excuse."* Just by seeing all these things, we can see the power and the divine nature of God the Creator who is the origin of all things.

If men try to understand God within the scope of their own knowledge, they definitely will have a limit. That is why many people do not believe the words written in the Bible. Also, some say they believe but they do not believe all the words of the Bible completely. Because Jesus knew this situation of men, He confirmed the word that He preached with so many powerful works. He said, *"Unless you people see signs and wonders, you simply will not believe"* (John 4:48).

It's the same today. God is almighty. If we believe in this almighty God and completely rely on Him, any problem can be resolved and any disease can be healed.

God began to create all things with His Word saying, *"Let there be light."* When the original voice of the Creator God is spoken forth, the blind will come to see, and those who are in wheelchairs and on crutches will walk and leap. I hope you will receive the answers to all your prayers and wishes with faith when the original voice of God is spoken forth.

Emmanuel Marallano Yaipen (Lima, Peru)

Being set free from the fear of AIDS

I had a medical check-up to join the army in 2001, and I heard, "You're HIV positive." It was completely unexpected news. I felt cursed.

I didn't take the frequent diarrhea too seriously.

I just sat in the chair and I felt so helpless.

'How can I tell my mother about this?'

I was in pain, but my heart was broken even more thinking about my mother. I had diarrhea more frequently, and there was mold in my mouth and fingertips. My fear of death began increasingly seizing me little by little.
But then I heard there was a powerful servant of God from South

Korea coming to Peru in December 2004. But I couldn't believe my disease would be healed.

I gave up, but my grandmother strongly urged me to attend the crusade. Eventually I went to 'Campo de Marte' where the '2004 Peru United Crusade with Rev. Dr. Jaerock Lee' was held. I wanted to hold on to this last hope.

My body was already thrilled by the power of the Holy Spirit while listening to the message. The works of the Holy Spirit manifested were a series of miracles.

Rev. Dr. Jaerock Lee did not pray for each individual, but he just prayed for the whole crowd. And yet so many people testified that they were healed. Many people stood up from wheelchairs and threw away their crutches. Many were rejoicing for their incurable diseases were healed.

A miracle happened to me, too. I went to the bathroom after the crusade was over, and for the first time in a long time I urinated

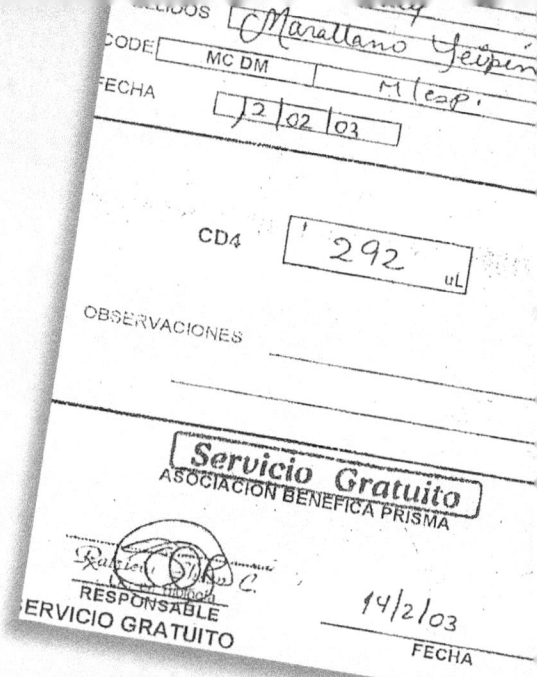

normally. My diarrhea stopped in two and a half months. My body felt so light. I was sure that I was healed and I went to the hospital. The diagnosis said CD4 immune cell count increased so dramatically that it was in the normal range.

AIDS is an incurable disease which is called the modern Black Death. The HIV keeps on destroying the CD4 immune cells. This leads to the extremely low immune function which will cause other complications, and eventual death.
The CD4 immune cells were dying, and it is truly amazing that they were recovered by the prayer of Rev. Dr. Jaerock Lee.

- Extract from *Extraordinary Things* -

Chapter 2 Heavens

> The original God dwells in the fourth heaven,
> governing all the heavens,
> the first heaven, the second heaven,
> and the third heaven.

The many heavens

The first heaven and the second heaven

Garden of Eden

The third heaven

The fourth heaven, the dwelling space of God

God the Creator, the Almighty

God the Almighty transcends human limitations

To meet the almighty God the Creator

"You alone are the LORD. You have made the heavens,
the heaven of heavens with all their host,
the earth and all that is on it, the seas and all that is in them.
You give life to all of them
and the heavenly host bows down before You."

Nehemiah 9:6

God is beyond human limitations. He exists from before eternity throughout eternity. The world that He lives in is a space of which the dimension is completely different from that of this world. The visible world that men live in is the physical realm, and the space where God dwells is a spiritual realm. The spiritual realm definitely exists, but only because it is not visible to our physical eyes, people tend to deny its existence.

A certain astronaut in the past said, "I traveled the universe but God was not there." What a foolish remark it is! He thinks the visible universe is all there is. But even the astronomers are merely able to say even this visible universe is limitless. And how much of this vast universe had that astronaut seen that he could deny the existence of God? Having human limitations, we cannot even explain all the things just in the universe we are living in.

The many heavens

Nehemiah 9:6 says, *"You alone are the LORD. You have made the heavens, the heaven of heavens with all their host, the earth and all that is on it, the seas and all that is in them. You give life to all of them and the heavenly host bows down before You."* It tells us that there is not just one heaven but many heavens.

Then, how many heavens are there actually? If you believe in the kingdom of heaven, you probably can think of two heavens. One is the sky in this physical realm, and the other in the kingdom of heaven that is the heaven of the spiritual realm. But the Bible mentions multiple numbers of heavens in many places.

> "To Him who rides upon the highest heavens, which are from ancient times; behold, He speaks forth with His voice, a mighty voice" (Psalm 68:33).

> "But will God indeed dwell on the earth? Behold, heaven and the highest heaven cannot contain You, how much less this house which I have built!" (1 Kings 8:27)

> "I know a man in Christ who fourteen years ago -- whether in the body I do not know, or out of the body I do not know, God knows -- such a man was caught up to the third heaven" (2 Corinthians 12:2).

The apostle Paul being taken to the third heaven tells us that there are the first, the second, and the third heavens, and there could be more heavens too.

Also, Stephen said in Acts 7:56, *"Behold, I see the heavens opened up and the Son of Man standing at the right hand of God."* If men's spiritual eyes are opened, they are able to see the spiritual realm and realize the existence of the kingdom of heaven.

Today, even scientists say there are many skies. One of the leading scientists in this subject is Max Tegmark, a cosmologist, who introduced the concept of a four-level multiverse.

It basically says that, based on the cosmological observations, our universe is a part of the whole universe where multiple universes exist, and each universe might have completely different physical characteristics.

The different physical characteristics mean that the characteristics of time and space could be very different. Of course, science cannot explain everything about spiritual realm. However, even with scientific approach, we can at least get the glimpse of the fact that our universe is not all there is.

The first heaven and the second heaven

The many heavens can be categorized generally into two sub-categories. They are the heaven in the spiritual realm which is invisible to our eyes and the heaven in the physical realm that we are living in. The physical universe we are living in is the first heaven and from the second heaven onward is the spiritual realm. In the second heaven there is the area of light where the Garden of Eden is located and the area of darkness where the evil spirits dwell.

Ephesians 2:2 says the evil spirits are 'the prince of the power of the air,' and this 'air' belongs to the second heaven. Genesis 3:24 tells us that at the east of the Garden of Eden God stationed the cherubim and the flaming sword which turned every direction to guard the way to the tree of life.

> "So He drove the man out; and at the east of the garden of Eden He stationed the cherubim and the flaming sword which turned every direction to guard the way to the tree of life."

Now, why would God station them at the east? It is because 'east' is like the borderline between the world of evil spirits and the Garden of Eden that belongs to God. God guarded the Garden to prevent the evil spirits from possibly penetrating into the Garden, eating from the tree of life and gaining eternal life.

Before he ate from the tree of the knowledge of good and evil, Adam had had the authority which he had received from God to rule over the Garden of Eden and all things in the first heaven. But Adam was driven out from the Garden because he disobeyed the Word of God and ate from the tree of knowledge. From then on, somebody else needed to guard the Garden of Eden where the tree of life was located. That is why God stationed the cherubim and the flaming sword that turned in every direction in the place of Adam in order to guard the Garden.

Garden of Eden

In Genesis chapter 2, after God created Adam from the dust on this earth, He made a garden in Eden and brought Adam into that place. Adam was a 'living being' or 'living spirit'. He was a spiritual being who received the breath of life from God. That is why God brought him into the second heaven, which is a spiritual space, for him to live there.

God also blessed him to subdue and rule over everything, while traveling to the Earth in the first heaven. But after Adam sinned with his disobedience to God, his spirit died and he could no longer live in a spiritual space. That is why he was driven out to the Earth.

And those who do not understand this fact still try to find the Garden of Eden on the Earth. It's because they do not understand that the Garden of Eden is located in the second heaven, spiritual realm, and not in this physical world.

Pyramids in Giza, Egypt, one of the wonders of the world, are so sophisticated and grand even to the extent that they look like they were not built by human technology. The average weight of each piece of the stone is 2.5 tons. And 2.3 million pieces of stone make up a pyramid. Where did they get all these stones? Also, what kinds of tools did they use to build them at that time?

Then who built these pyramids? The question can be answered easily if we understand about many heavens and spiritual space. More details are explained in the Genesis lectures. Now, after Adam was driven out from the Garden of Eden due to his disobedience, who lives in the Garden?

In Genesis 3:16, God told Eve after she committed a sin, *"I will greatly multiply your pain in childbirth, in pain you will bring forth children."* 'Multiply' means there had been some pain in childbirth and it was going to be greatly increased. Also, Genesis 1:28 tells us that Adam and Eve 'multiplied', meaning that Eve gave birth while living in the Garden of Eden.

Therefore, the number of children Adam and Eve had in the Garden of Eden was countless. And, they are still living there even after Adam and Eve were driven out due to their sins. It's just that before Adam sinned, people in the Garden of Eden could travel to the Earth freely, but restrictions were made after Adam was driven out.

The concept of time and space between the first heaven and the second heaven is very different. There is a flow of time in the second heaven, too, but it is not as limited as the first heaven, our physical world. In the Garden of Eden, nobody ages or dies. Nothing perishes or becomes extinct. Even after a long time, people in the Garden of Eden do not feel so much of the difference in time. They feel as if they were living in time that is not flowing. Also, the space in Eden is limitless.

If people do not die in the first heaven, it would be full of people someday. But because the second heaven has limitless space, it will never be full of people no matter how many people are born.

The third heaven

There is another heaven that belongs to the spiritual realm. It is the third heaven, where the kingdom of heaven is located. It is the place where the saved children of God will live forever. The apostle Paul received clear revelations and visions from the Lord, and he said in 2 Corinthians 12:2-4, *"I know a man in Christ who fourteen years ago—whether in the body I do not know, or out of the body I do not know, God knows—such a man was caught up to the third heaven. And I know how such a man—whether in the body or apart from the body I do not know, God knows—was caught up into Paradise and heard inexpressible words, which a man is not permitted to speak."*

Just as there is the capital city for each country and other smaller cities and even small towns, there are many dwelling places in the kingdom of heaven as well beginning from the city of New Jerusalem, where the throne of God is located, to Paradise which can be considered as the outskirts of the kingdom of heaven. Our dwelling places will be different depending on how much we loved God and the extent to which we cultivated the heart of truth and recovered the lost image of God on this earth.

The third heaven has even less limitations of time and space than the second heaven. It has eternal time and endless space. It is difficult for human beings, who are living in the first heaven, to understand the space and time of the kingdom of heaven. Let's think of a balloon. Before you blow air into it, the balloon's area and volume is limited. But it can change drastically depending on the amount of air you blow into it. The space in the kingdom of heaven is similar. When we build a house on this earth, we need a piece of land, and the space we can create on that land will be limited. But in the space of the third heaven, houses can be built in a very different way than that of this earth because the concept of area, volume, length, or height there is beyond those of this earth.

The fourth heaven, the dwelling space of God

The fourth heaven is the original space where God existed before the beginning, before He divided the entire universe into several heavens. In the fourth heaven, it is meaningless to use the conception of time and space. The fourth heaven transcends every concept of time and space, and in that place anything that God desires in His mind will be done immediately as it is.

The resurrected Lord appeared to His disciples who were afraid of the Jews and were hiding in the house with all the doors locked (John 20:19-29). He appeared in the middle of the house even though nobody opened any door for Him. He also appeared out of nowhere to His disciples who were at Galilee and ate with them (John 21:1-14). He was here on this earth for forty days and ascended into Heaven through the clouds in the sight of many people. We can see the resurrected Jesus Christ could transcend physical space and time.

Then, how much more so would things be in the fourth heaven where the God in origin once dwelt? Just as He harbored and governed all the spaces in the universe while existing as the Light containing the Voice, He rules over all of the first heaven, second heaven, and third heavens while dwelling in the fourth heaven.

God the Creator, the Almighty

This world where human beings live is a very small speck compared with the other spacious and mysterious heavens. On the earth, men do everything possible to live a better life going through all kinds of hardships and difficulties. For them things on this earth are so complex and problems are difficult to solve, but none of them pose a problem to God.

Suppose a man is watching the world of ants. Sometimes ants have great difficulty carrying food. But a man can put it into the ants' house so easily. If an ant meets a puddle too big for it to cross, the man can hold it in his hand and transfer it to the ground on the other side. However difficult any problem may be for the ants, it is a small thing to a man. Likewise, with the help of God the Almighty, nothing can be a problem.

The Old Testament testifies to the almightiness of God so many times. With the almighty power of God, the Red Sea was parted and the flooding Jordan River stopped. The sun and the moon stood still, and when Moses struck a rock with his staff, water sprang out from it. No matter how great power and riches and how much knowledge a man may have, is it possible for him to part a sea and stop the sun and the moon? But Jesus said in Mark 10:27, *"With people it is impossible, but not with God; for all things are possible with God."*

The New Testament also presents many cases where the sick

and the disabled were healed and made complete and even the dead were brought back to life by the power of God. When handkerchiefs or aprons that had touched Paul were taken to the sick, the diseases left and the evil spirits departed.

God the Almighty transcends human limitations

Even today, if we can just get the help of the power of God, nothing will be a problem. Even the seemingly most difficult problems will no longer be problems. And this is proven every week in the church I am ministering. So many incurable diseases including AIDS were healed as the believers listen to the Word of God in worship services and receive the prayer of healing.

Not just in South Korea but also countless people around the world have experienced the amazing healing works that are written in the Bible. Such works were once introduced by CNN. Additionally, we have assistant pastors who pray with the handkerchiefs on which I prayed. Through such prayers, astonishing works of divine healing take place transcending the races and cultures.

As for me, too, all my life's problems were solved after I met God the Creator. So many diseases covered me that I was nicknamed "a diseases' department store." There was no peace in the family. I couldn't see a single ray of hope. But I was healed of all my diseases the moment I knelt down in a church. God blessed me to repay the financial debts I owed. It was so large that it seemed impossible to pay back in my life-time, but it was repaid in just several months. My family recovered happiness and joy. Above all, God gave me a calling to become a pastor and gave me His power to save numerous souls.

Today so many people say they believe in God, but there are very few who live with true faith. If they have a problem, most of them rely on human ways rather than depending on God. They are frustrated and discouraged when their problems are not solved with their own ways. If they fall ill, they do not look to God, but depend on doctors in a hospital. If they face hardships in their business, they seek for help here and there.

Some believers complain to God or lose faith because of physical hardships. They become unstable in their faith and lose fullness if they are persecuted or when they expect some loss due to walking uprightly. However, if they believe God created all the heavens and He makes everything possible, certainly they will not do that.

God created all kinds of internal organs of human beings. Is there any kind of serious disease God cannot heal? God said, *"The silver is Mine and the gold is Mine"* (Haggai 2:8). Can He not make His children rich? God can do everything, but men feel discouraged or disheartened and depart from the truth because they do not trust God the Almighty. No matter what kind of problem one has, he can solve it any time if he really trusts God from his heart and relies on Him.

To meet the almighty God the Creator

The story of the commander Naaman in 2 Kings Chapter 5 teaches us how to receive the answers to our problems from God the Almighty. Naaman was the commander of the army of Aram, but could not do anything about his leprosy.

One day he heard from a little Hebrew maidservant about the power of God that Elisha the prophet of Israel had performed. He was a Gentile man who did not believe in God, but did not neglect the little girl's words because he had a good heart. He prepared valuable offerings to meet Elisha, the man of God, and started a long trip.

But when he came to the house of Elisha, the prophet neither prayed for him nor welcomed him. All the prophet did was to let a servant convey a message to him to wash his body in Jordan River seven times. At first he felt offended, but it was not long before he changed his mind and obeyed. Although neither the deeds nor the words of Elisha made sense in his way of thinking, he trusted and obeyed because God's prophet who had performed with the power of God spoke the words.

When Naaman dipped himself into the Jordan seven times, his leprosy was miraculously and completely healed. Here, what does dipping his body into the Jordan symbolize? Water is the Word of God. It means one can be forgiven of his sins if he cleanses the dirty things of his heart with the Word of God, the way he cleans his body with water. Because the number of seven stands for perfection, dipping seven times indicates that he was completely forgiven.

As explained, for us men to receive the answer from the almighty God, the passageway of communication must be opened between God and us by being forgiven of our sins. It says in Isaiah 59:1-2, *"Behold, the LORD's hand is not so short that it cannot save; nor is His ear so dull that it cannot hear. But your iniquities have made a separation between you and your God, and your sins have hidden His face from you so that He does not hear."*

If we did not know God and have not accepted Jesus Christ, we have to repent of not having accepted Jesus Christ (John 16:9). God says we are murderers if we hate our brothers (1 John 3:15), and we have to repent that we have not loved our brothers. James 4:2-3 says, *"You lust and do not have; so you commit murder. You are envious and cannot obtain; so you fight and quarrel. You do not have because you do not ask. You ask and do not receive, because you ask with wrong motives, so that you may spend it on your pleasures."* Thus, we have to repent of praying with greed and praying with doubt (James 1:6-7).

Furthermore, if we did not put the Word of God into practice while professing our faith, we have to repent thoroughly. We should not just say we are sorry. We have to rend our hearts completely while shedding tears with a runny nose. Our repentance can be considered true repentance only when we have firm determination to live by the Word of God and actually practice it.

Deuteronomy 32:39 says, *"See now that I, I am He, and there is no god besides Me; it is I who put to death and give life. I have wounded and it is I who heal, and there is no one who can deliver from My hand."* This is the God whom we believe in.

God created all heavens and all things in them. He knows all our situations. He is powerful enough to answer all our prayers. No matter how desperate or depressing the situations are for men, He can turn everything around like flipping a coin. Therefore, I hope you will receive answers to prayers and hearts' desires by having true faith to rely on God only.

Dr. Vitaliy Fishberg (New York City, United States)

At the scene of Miracles

Before I graduated from Moldova medical school, I was the editor-in-chief of a medical journal, 'Your Family Doctor', which is renowned in Moldova, Ukraine, Russia, and Belarus. In 1997, I moved to the USA. I did doctorate in Naturopathic Medicine, PHD in Clinical Nutrition and Integrative Medicine, Doctorate in Alternative Medicine, Doctorate in Orthomolecular Medicine and honorary Doctorate in Natural Health Science. When I came to New York after my education, very soon I became really famous in Russian community and many newspapers published my articles every week. In 2006, I heard there would be a big Christian meeting in Madison Square Garden. I had a chance to meet with a delegation of Manmin church, and I felt the power of the Holy Spirit through them. Two weeks later I attended the crusade.

Rev. Dr. Jaerock Lee prayed for the attendants after preaching about why Jesus is our Savior. "**Lord, heal them! Father, God, if the message I preached is not true, let me not perform any powerful works tonight! But if it is true, let so many souls see the evidence** of the living God. Let the lame walk! Let those who can't hear, hear! All incurable diseases, be burnt by the fire of the Holy Spirit and be healthy!"

I was shocked to hear such a prayer. What if no divine healing took place? How could he so confidently pray the way he did? But amazing things were already happening even before the prayer for the sick ended. People who were suffering from evil spirits were set free. The mute came to speak. The blind came to see. So many people testified of their hearing impairment being healed. Many people stood up from wheelchairs and threw away their crutches. Some of them testified they were healed of AIDS.

As the crusade progressed, God's power was displayed more greatly. Doctors of World Christian Doctors Network, WCDN, who came from many countries, set up a table to receive the testimonies. They tried to medically verify the testimonies, and towards the end, we ran short of doctors who could register all the people testifying to their healing!

Nubia Cano, a 54-year-old lady living in Queens was diagnosed with vertebral cancer in 2003. She'd been unable to move about or walk. She spent all of her time in bed and the excruciating pain forced her to take morphine injections every 2 hours. The doctor told her she wouldn't be able to walk again.
When she attended "The 2006 New York Crusade with Rev. Dr. Jaerock Lee" with a friend, she saw many people were receiving God's healing, and she began to gain faith. When she received Rev. Lee's prayer, she felt warmth throughout her body and felt like someone was massaging her back. The pain in the back went away and ever since the crusade, she's been able to walk and bend her waist! Her

Medical doctors of WCDN verifying testimonies

doctor was simply astonished to see her—someone who was never to walk again—walk as freely as ever. She can even dance to the tunes of Merengue now.

Maximillia Rodriguez living in Brooklyn had very poor eyesight. She'd been wearing contact lenses for 14 years and eyeglasses for the last 2 years. On the last day of the crusade, she received Rev. Dr. Jaerock Lee's prayer by faith and immediately realized that she could begin to see without her glasses. Today, she can read even the finest prints in her Bible without the aid of her eyeglasses. Her ophthalmologist, after noticing and confirming an undeniable improvement in her eyesight, could only be amazed at what he was witnessing.

Madison Square Garden, where the crusade was held in July 2006, was truly a scene of miracles. I was so moved witnessing the power of God. His power changed me and let me see a new course of life. I made up my mind to become God's instrument to medically prove God's healing works and make them known all over the world.

- Extract from *Extraordinary Things* -

Chapter 3 Triune God

> The God we believe in is one God.
> But He has three persons in Him:
> the Father, the Son, and the Holy Spirit.

The providence of God for human cultivation

The nature and the order of God the Trinity

The roles of God the Trinity

Jesus the Son opens the way of salvation

Holy Spirit completes salvation

Do not quench the Spirit

God the Father, the Director of human cultivation

The Triune God fulfills the providence of salvation

Denying the Triune God and works of the Holy Spirit

"Go therefore and make disciples of all the nations, baptizing them in the name of the Father and the Son and the Holy Spirit."

Matthew 28:19

God the Trinity means that God the Father, God the Son, and God the Holy Spirit are one. The God we believe in is one God. But He has Three Persons in Him: the Father, the Son, and the Holy Spirit. And yet, because They are one, we say 'Triune God' or 'God the Trinity'.

This is a very important doctrine of Christianity, but there is hardly anybody who can explain about it accurately and in detail. It's because it is very difficult for men, who have limited thinking and theories, to understand the origin of God the Creator. But to the extent that we understand God the Trinity, we can understand His heart and will more clearly and receive blessings and answers to our prayers in communication with Him.

The providence of God for human cultivation

God said in Exodus 3:14, *"I AM WHO I AM."* Nobody gave birth to Him or created Him. He just existed from the beginning. He is beyond men's understanding or imagination; He has no beginning or end; He just exists from before eternity throughout eternity. As explained above, God existed alone as the Light with the chiming voice within in the vast space (John 1:1; 1 John 1:5). But at a certain point in time He wanted to have somebody with whom He could share love, and He planned human cultivation to gain true children.

To conduct human cultivation, God first divided the space. He divided the space into a spiritual space and the physical space where people with physical bodies would live. After that, He came to exist as the Triune God. The original God came to exist in three persons of the Father, the Son, and the Holy Spirit.

The Bible says that God the Son Jesus Christ was born of God (Acts 13:33), and John 15:26 and Galatians 4:6 say the Holy Spirit also came out from God. Like creating an alter ego, the Son Jesus and the Holy Spirit proceeded from God the Father. This was absolutely necessary for human cultivation.

Jesus the Son and the Holy Spirit are not creatures who were created by God, but They are the original God Himself. They are one in origin, but They exist independently for human cultivation. Their roles are different but They are one in heart, thoughts, and power, and that is why we say They are God the Trinity.

The nature and the order of God the Trinity

Like God the Father, Jesus the Son and the Holy Spirit are almighty, too. Also, Jesus the Son and the Holy Spirit feel and desire what God the Father feels and desires. Reversely, God the Father feels the joy and pains of Jesus the Son and the Holy Spirit. And yet, the Three Persons are independent entities who have independent characters and Their roles are also different.

On the one hand, Jesus the Son has received the same heart of God the Father, but His divinity is stronger than His humanity. Thus His divine dignity and justice are more prominent. On the other hand, in case of the Holy Spirit, His humanity is stronger. His delicate, kind, merciful, and compassionate characters are more prominent.

As explained, God the Son and God the Holy Spirit are one

in origin with God the Father but are independent entities with well distinguishable characters. Their roles are also different according to the order. After God the Father is the Son Jesus Christ and the Holy Spirit is after the Son. He serves the Son and the Father with love.

The roles of God the Trinity

The Three Persons of the Trinity conduct the ministry of human cultivation together. Each of the Three Persons fully plays His own part, but They sometimes did the ministry together at very important points in human cultivation.

For example, Genesis 1:26 says, *"Then God said, 'Let Us make man in Our image, according to Our likeness;"* We can infer that God the Trinity together created human beings in Their likeness. Also, when God came down to inspect the Tower of Babel, the Three Persons was in company. When people began to build the Tower of Babel with the desire to become like God, God the Trinity confused their language.

It is said in Genesis 11:7, *"Come, let Us go down and there confuse their language, so that they will not understand one another's speech."* Here, 'Us' is first person plural pronoun, and we can see the Three Persons of God the Trinity were together. As explained, the Three Persons sometimes worked as one, but actually They perform separate roles so that the providence of human cultivation would be completed beginning from the Creation up to the salvation of human beings. Now, what role does each Person of the Trinity have respectively?

Jesus the Son opens the way of salvation

The role of the Son Jesus is to become the Savior and to open the way of salvation for sinners. Since Adam in disobedience ate the fruit that was forbidden by God, sin came into human beings. Now, human beings were in need of salvation.

And they were doomed to fall into everlasting death, the fire of Hell, according to the law of the spiritual realm saying that the wages of sin is death. However, Jesus, the Son of God, paid the penalty of death for sinners so that they might not fall into Hell.

Now, why did Jesus the Son have to become the Savior of all mankind? Just as each country has its own law, so the spiritual realm has its own law, and not just anybody can become the Savior. One can open the way of salvation only when he meets all the qualifications. What, then, are the qualifications to become the Savior and open the way of salvation for the mankind who were doomed to death due to sins?

First of all, the Savior must be a man. 1 Corinthians 15:21 says, *"For since by a man came death, by a man also came the resurrection of the dead."* As written, because death came into men due to the disobedience of the man Adam, salvation must also come through a man like Adam.

Second, the Savior must not be a descendant of Adam. Adam's descendants are all sinners who are born with the original sin inherited from their fathers. No descendant of Adam can become the Savior. But Jesus was conceived by the Holy Spirit, and He is not a descendant of Adam. He does not have any original sin inherited from parents (Matthew 1:18-21).

Third, the Savior must have power. In order to redeem sinners from the enemy devil, the Savior must have the power, and spiritual power is to be sinless. He must not have original sin, and He must not commit any sin obeying thoroughly the Word of God. He must be free of any blemish or spot.

Lastly, the Savior must have love. Even if one has all the three qualifications above, he would not die for the sin of other people if he has no love. Then, mankind would never be saved. Thus, the Savior must have the love to take the punishment of death in place of the mankind who are sinners.

The movie, 'The Passion of the Christ' depicted the sufferings of Jesus very well. Jesus was flogged and His flesh was ripped open. He was nailed through His hands and feet and He wore the thorns on His head. He was hung on a cross and when He finally breathed His last, He was pierced on His side and He shed all His water and blood. He took all those sufferings to redeem us from all our iniquities, sins, diseases, and weaknesses.

Since Adam's sin, no human has met all four qualifications. Foremost, Adam's descendants inherit the original sin, namely the sinful nature from their ancestors when they are born. And there is no man who has lived completely according to the law of God and there is no one who has not sinned at all. A man in a great debt cannot pay off the debt of others. In the same manner, sinners who have original sin and self-committed sins cannot save sinners, other human beings. For this reason God prepared the secret hidden since before the ages, namely Jesus the Son of God.

Jesus has met all the qualifications of the Savior. He was born on the earth with the flesh of a man, but was not conceived by the combination of a sperm of a man and an egg of a woman. The Virgin Mary was with child by the Holy Spirit. So, Jesus was not a descendant of Adam and had no original sin. And, throughout His entire life He fully obeyed the Law and did not commit any personal sin at all.

This perfectly qualified Jesus was crucified with sacrificing love for sinners. And thus, human beings gained the way to be forgiven of their sins through His blood. If Jesus had not become the Savior, all human beings since Adam would have fallen into Hell. Also, if everyone had fallen into Hell, the goal of human cultivation would not have been achieved. This means that nobody would have been able to enter the kingdom of heaven and accordingly God would not have gained any true children.

That is why God prepared Jesus the Son who would perform the role of the Savior, in order to fulfill the purpose of human cultivation. Anybody who believes in Jesus, who died on the cross for us without any sin, can be forgiven of his sins and receive the right to become a child of God.

Holy Spirit completes salvation

Next, the part of the Holy Spirit is to complete the salvation that people gained through Jesus the Son. It is like the mother would nurse and raise a new born baby. The Holy Spirit plants faith in the hearts of those who accept the Lord and lead them until they reach the kingdom of heaven. He divides countless spirits when He does His ministry. The original entity of the Holy Spirit is at one place, but countless spirits divided from

Him do the ministries at the same time anywhere in the world with the same heart and power.

Of course, the Father and the Son can divide countless spirits as in the case of the Holy Spirit. Jesus said in Matthew 18:20, *"For where two or three have gathered together in My name, I am there in their midst."* We can understand that Jesus can divide numerous spirits from His original person. The Lord Jesus cannot be with believers as His original person at every place where they gather in His name. Instead, His divided spirits go everywhere and are with them.

The Holy Spirit leads every believer as kindly and lovingly as a nursing mother cares her baby. When people accept the Lord, the spirits divided from the Holy Spirit come into their hearts. No matter how many people accept the Lord, the Holy Spirit's divided spirits can come into the hearts of all of them and dwell therein. When this happens, we say they 'received the Holy Spirit'. The Holy Spirit dwelling in the hearts of believers helps them have the spiritual faith to be saved, and He trains their faith to grow up to the full measure like a private teacher.

He leads the believers to diligently learn the Word of God, to change their heart according to the Word, and to keep on growing up spiritually. According to the Word of God, believers have to change hot-temperedness into meekness, and hatred into love. If you had envy or jealousy in the past, now you must rejoice in the success of others in truth. If you were arrogant, now you must be humble and serve others.

If you sought your own benefits in the past, now you must sacrifice yourself to the point of death. To the people who do evil deeds toward you, you must not do evil to them but move their hearts with goodness.

Do not quench the Spirit

Even after you accepted the Lord and have been a believer for several years, if you still live the untruth just as when you were a non-believer, the Holy Spirit dwelling within you will groan very much. If we are easily irritated when we suffer without a reason, or if we pass judgment and condemnation on our brothers in Christ and reveal their transgressions, we wouldn't be able to lift up our head before the Lord who died for our sins.

Suppose you have gained a church title such as that of a deacon or elder, but you do not have peace with others or give others a hard time, or make them stumble by being self-righteous. Then, the Holy Spirit dwelling within you will grieve so much. Since we accepted the Lord and were born again, we must try to cast away every kind of evil and sin and to increase our faith day after day.

Even after accepting the Lord, if you still live in sins of the world and commit the sins leading to death, the Holy Spirit in you will eventually leave you, and your name will be blotted out from the book of life. Exodus 32:33 says, *"The LORD said to Moses, 'Whoever has sinned against Me, I will blot him out of My book.'"*

Revelation 3:5 says, *"He who overcomes will thus be clothed in white garments; and I will not erase his name from the book of life, and I will confess his name before My Father and before His angels."* These verses tell us, even if we have received the Holy Spirit and our names have been written in the book of life, they can be erased, too.

Also, 1 Thessalonians 5:19 says, *"Do not quench the Spirit."* As said, even though you are saved and have received the Holy Spirit, if you do not live in the truth, the Holy Spirit will be quenched.

The Holy Spirit dwells in the heart of each believer and leads him not to lose salvation by continually enlightening him about the truth and urging him to live according to the will of God. While teaching us about sin and righteousness He lets us know that God is the Creator, Jesus Christ is our Savior, there is Heaven and Hell, and there will be the Judgment.

The Holy Spirit intercedes for us before God the Father just as it is written in Romans 8:26, *"In the same way the Spirit also helps our weakness; for we do not know how to pray as we should, but the Spirit Himself intercedes for us with groanings too deep for words."* He laments when children of God commit sins, and helps them to repent and turn from their ways.

And He pours down on them the inspiration and fullness of the Holy Spirit and gives them various gifts so that they can throw away all kinds of sins and experience the works of God. We who are children of God must ask for these works of the Holy Spirit and long for the deeper things.

God the Father, the Director of human cultivation

God the Father is the director of the great plan for human cultivation. He is the Creator, Ruler, and the Judge on the Last Day. God the Son, Jesus Christ, opened the way for saving human beings who are sinners. Finally, God the Holy Spirit guides those who are saved to have true faith and to reach complete salvation. In other words, the Holy Spirit completes the salvation given to each believer. Each ministry of the Three Persons of God acts as one power in achieving the providence of cultivating human beings as true children.

However, each of Their ministries is strictly distinguished according to the order, yet the Three Persons work in concert at the same time. When Jesus came down to the earth, He completely followed the will of the Father without asserting His own will. The Holy Spirit was with Jesus helping Him with His ministry, from the time Jesus was conceived in Virgin Mary. When Jesus was hung on the cross and suffered from pains, the Father and the Holy Spirit felt the same feeling and pain at the same time.

In the same way, when the Holy Spirit groans and intercedes for the souls, the Lord and the Father feel the same pain and lament too. The Three Persons of God the Trinity did everything with the same heart and will at every moment and felt the same emotions respectively in the ministry of each Person. In a word, the Three Persons have accomplished everything in Three in One.

The Triune God fulfills the providence of salvation

The Three Persons of God fulfill the providence of human cultivation as Three In One. It is said in 1 John 5:8, *"the Spirit and the water and the blood; and the three are in agreement."* The water here symbolizes the ministry of God the Father who is the Word. The blood stands for the ministry of the Lord who shed the blood on the cross. God the Trinity does the ministry as the Spirit, the Water, and the Blood who are in agreement, in order to testify that believing children are saved.

So, we must clearly understand each ministry of God the Trinity and must not incline toward only one Person of the Trinity. Only when we accept and believe the Three Persons of God the Trinity, will we be saved with the faith in God, and we will be able to say we know God. When we pray, we pray in the name of Jesus Christ, but it is the Father God who answers us, and it is the Holy Spirit who helps us receive the answer.

Jesus also said in Matthew 28:19, *"Go therefore and make disciples of all the nations, baptizing them in the name of the Father and the Son and the Holy Spirit,"* and the apostle Paul blessed the believers in the name of the Trinity in 2 Corinthians 13:14, *"The grace of the Lord Jesus Christ, and the love of God, and the fellowship of the Holy Spirit, be with you all."* That is why, in the Sunday morning services, the benediction is given so that the children of God will receive the grace of the Savior and Lord Jesus Christ, the love of God the Father, and the inspiration and fullness of the Holy Spirit.

Denying the Triune God and works of the Holy Spirit

There are some people who do not accept the Trinity. Among them is the Jehovah's Witnesses. They do not acknowledge the divinity of Jesus Christ. They also do not acknowledge the individual personality of the Holy Spirit, and thus they are considered heretical.

The Bible says those who deny Jesus Christ and bring swift destruction upon themselves are heretical (2 Peter 2:1). They look like they practice Christianity on the outside but they do not follow the will of God. They have nothing to do with salvation and we believers must not be deceived.

Different from those heresies, some churches deny the works of the Holy Spirit though they say they confess the faith of the Trinity. The Bible illustrates various gifts of the Holy Spirit such as speaking in tongues, prophecy, divine healing, revelations, and visions. And there are some churches that judge these works of the Holy Spirit as something wrong or try to hinder the works of the Holy Spirit, although they confess that they believe in God.

They often condemn the churches that manifest the gifts of the Holy Spirit as heretical. This directly offends the will of God, and they commit the unforgivable sin of blaspheming, disgracing, or opposing the Holy Spirit. When they commit these sins, the spirit of repentance does not come on them, and they cannot even repent.

And if they slander or condemn a servant of God or the church filled with the works of the Holy Spirit, it is the same as condemning God the Trinity and acting as the enemy standing against God. The children of God who are saved and have received the Holy Spirit must not avoid the works of the Holy Spirit, but quite to the contrary, they should long for those works. Especially ministers must not only experience the works of the Holy Spirit, but also perform those works of the Holy Spirit so that their flocks can live abundant lives by those works.

1 Corinthians 4:20 says, *"For the kingdom of God does not consist in words but in power."* If ministers teach their flock

only with knowledge or formalities, it means they are blind men guiding other blind men. Ministers must teach their flock the exact truth and let them experience the evidence of the living God by performing the works of the Holy Spirit.

Today is referred to as the 'Era of the Holy Spirit'. Under the leading guidance of the Holy Spirit, we receive the abundant blessings and grace of God the Trinity who cultivates human beings.

John 14:16-17 says, *"I will ask the Father, and He will give you another Helper, that He may be with you forever; that is the Spirit of truth, whom the world cannot receive, because it does not see Him or know Him, but you know Him because He abides with you and will be in you."*

After the Lord fulfilled the ministry of human salvation, resurrected, and ascended into Heaven, the Holy Spirit succeeded the Lord in the ministry of human cultivation. The Holy Spirit is with every believer who accepts the Lord and leads these believers to the truth dwelling in the heart of each believer.

Moreover, today as sins prevail and darkness increasingly covers the world, God shows Himself to those who search for Him from the heart, and gives them the fiery works of the Holy Spirit. I hope you will become true children of God in the works of the Father, the Son, and the Holy Spirit, so that you will receive everything you ask in prayer and reach complete salvation.

Examples of the Bible

Things that happened when the gate
of the second heaven opened
into the first heaven.

The first heaven is the physical space in which we are living.
In the second heaven are the area of light, Eden, and the area of darkness.
In the third heaven is the kingdom of heaven where we will live forever.
The fourth heaven is the space of the original God, which is exclusively for God the Trinity.

These 'heavens' are strictly separated, but each space is 'adjacent' to each other.
When necessary, the gate of the second heaven opens in the space of the first heaven where we are living now.
Sometimes, the space of the third heaven or the fourth heaven might open, too.

We can find many events where the things of the second heaven took place in this first heaven.
When the gate of the second heaven opens and objects of the Garden of Eden come out to the space of the first heaven, those who are living in the first heaven can touch and see those objects.

Judgment of Fire on Sodom and Gomorrah

Genesis 19:24 says, *"Then the LORD rained on Sodom and Gomorrah brimstone and fire from the LORD out of heaven."* Here, 'from the LORD out of heaven' means that God opened the gate of the space of the second heaven and brought down brimstone and fire from there.

It was the same at Mt. Carmel when Elijah confronted the 850 priests of the Gentile gods by bringing down the answer of fire. In 1 Kings 18:37-38 it says, *"'Answer me, O LORD, answer me, that this people may know that You, O LORD, are God, and that You have turned their heart back again.' Then the fire of the LORD fell and consumed the burnt offering and the wood and the stones and the dust, and licked up the water that was in the trench."* The fire of the second heaven can actually burn the objects of the first heaven.

The star that guided the three magi

Matthew 2:9 says, *"After hearing the king, they went their way; and the star, which they had seen in the east, went on before them until it came and stood over the place where the Child was."* A star of the second heaven appeared, and it repeated moving and stopping for a while. When the magi reached the destination, the star stopped there.

If this star is a star of the first heaven, it would have had a tremendous effect on the universe, for all the stars in the first heaven are moving in their own path in a very orderly manner. We can understand that the star that guided the three magi was not one of those in the first heaven. God moved a star in the second heaven so that it wouldn't have had any impact on the universe of the first heaven. God opened the space of the second heaven so that the magi could see this star.

Manna given to the sons of Israel

Exodus 16:4 says, *"Then the LORD said to Moses, 'Behold, I will rain bread from heaven for you; and the people shall go out and gather a day's portion every day, that I may test them, whether or not they will walk in My instruction.'"*

As He said He would 'rain bread from heaven', God gave manna to the sons of Israel while they were wandering in the wilderness for 40 years. Manna was like coriander seed, and its appearance like that of bdellium. Its taste was as the taste of cakes baked with oil. As explained, in the Bible, there are many records about the events that took place when the gate of the space of the second heaven opened in the first heaven.

Chapter 4 Justice

> We can solve any kind of problem
> and bring down blessings and answers to prayers
> when we understand the justice of God correctly
> and act according to it..

God's Justice

God keeps His justice without fail

Acting by the rules of justice of God

Two sides of justice

Higher dimensions of justice

Faith and obedience – the basic rules of justice

"He will bring forth your righteousness as the light and your judgment as the noonday."

Psalm 37:6

There are problems that cannot be resolved by any human method. But they can go away in a moment if God just harbors them in His heart.

For example, about certain problems in mathematics that elementary school students find very difficult to solve, they are nothing for college students. In the same way, for God there is nothing impossible, because He is the Governor of all heavens.

In order to experience the power of the almighty God, we have to know the ways to receive answers from God and practice them. We can solve any problem and bring down answers and blessings when we understand the justice of God correctly and act according to it.

God's Justice

Justice refers to the rules that God has set, and those rules being precisely carried out. More simply put, it is like the rule of 'cause-and-effect'. There are rules that make certain causes bring about certain results.

Even the unbelievers say we reap what we sow. A Korean saying goes, "You reap beans where you sow beans, and you reap red beans where you sow red beans." As there are rules like these, the rules of justice are much stricter in the truth of God.

The Bible says, *"Ask, and it will be given to you; seek, and you will find; knock, and it will be opened to you"* (Matthew 7:7). *"Do not be deceived, God is not mocked; for whatever a man sows, this he will also reap"* (Galatians 6:7). *"Now this I say, he who sows sparingly will also reap sparingly, and he who sows bountifully will also reap bountifully"* (2 Corinthians 9:6). These are just a few examples of the rules of justice.

Also, there are rules about consequences of sins. Romans 6:23 says, *"For the wages of sin is death, but the free gift of God is eternal life in Christ Jesus our Lord."* Proverbs 16:18 says, *"Pride goes before destruction, and a haughty spirit before stumbling."* James 1:15 says, *"Then when lust has conceived, it gives birth to sin; and when sin is accomplished, it brings forth death."*

Other than these rules, there are also rules that unbelievers cannot really understand. For example, Matthew 23:11 says, *"But the greatest among you shall be your servant."* Matthew 10:39 says, *"He who has found his life will lose it, and he who has lost his life for My sake will find it."* Acts 20:35 latter part says, *"It is more blessed to give than to receive."* Let alone understanding them, unbelievers even think these rules are wrong.

But the Word of God is never wrong and it never changes. The truth that the world talks about changes with the passage of time, but the words of God written in the Bible, namely the rules of justice, are fulfilled as written.

Therefore, if we can correctly understand the justice of God, we can find the causes when there is any problem and solve it. Similarly we can also receive the answers to our hearts' desires. The Bible explains the reasons why we get a disease, why we suffer from financial problems, why there is no peace in our family, or why we lose the grace of God and stumble.

If we just understand the rules of justice written in the Bible, we can receive blessings and answers to our prayers. God faithfully keeps all the rules that He Himself had established, and therefore, if we just act according to them, we will definitely receive blessings and answers to problems.

God keeps His justice without fail

God is the Creator and Governor of all things, and yet He never violates the rules of justice. He never says, "I made those rules, but I don't have to keep them." He works in everything exactly according to justice, without any error.

It was to redeem us from our sins exactly according to the rules of justice that the Son of God, Jesus, came down to this earth and died on the cross.

Some might say, "Why can't God just destroy the devil and save everybody?" But He will never do that. He established rules of justice as He was making the plan of human cultivation in the beginning, and He keeps them as they are. That is why He made such a great sacrifice as giving even His only begotten Son to open the way of salvation for us.

Therefore, we cannot be saved and go to Heaven by just confessing, "I believe!" with our lips and going to church. We have to be within the boundaries of salvation which are set by God. In order for us to be saved we have to believe in Jesus Christ as our personal Savior and obey the Word of God by living according to the rules of justice.

Other than this matter of salvation, there are many parts of the Bible that explain to us the justice of God, who fulfills everything exactly according to the law of the spiritual realm. If we can understand this justice, it will be very easy for us to solve the problems of our sins. It will make it easier to receive blessings and answers to prayers as well. For example, what must you do if you want to receive your hearts' desires?

Psalm 37:4 says, *"Delight yourself in the LORD; and He will give you the desires of your heart."* To be able to really delight yourself in God, you first have to please God. And we can find many ways to please God in many parts of the Bible.

The first part of Hebrews 11:6 says, *"And without faith it is impossible to please Him."* We can please God to the extent that we believe in the Word of God, cast away sins, and become sanctified. Also, we can please God with our efforts and offerings like King Solomon who gave one thousand sacrifices. We can also do voluntary works for God's kingdom. There could be many other ways.

Therefore, we should understand that reading the Bible and listening to sermons is one of the ways to learn the rules of justice. If we just follow those rules and please God, we can receive all our hearts' desires and give glory to God.

Acting by the rules of justice of God

Since I accepted the Lord and realized the justice of God, it was great pleasure to lead a life in faith. As I acted according to the rules of justice, I received love of God and financial blessings.

Also, God says He would protect us from diseases and disasters if we live in the Word of God. And as I and my family members have been living only with faith, all my family members have been so healthy that we have never been to any hospital or taken any medicines since I accepted the Lord.

Because I believed the justice of God letting us reap what we sow, I enjoyed giving to God even though I was living a poor life. Some people say, "I am so poor that I don't have anything to give to God." But I gave more diligently because I was poor.

2 Corinthians 9:7 says, *"Each one must do just as he has purposed in his heart, not grudgingly or under compulsion, for God loves a cheerful giver."* As said, I never came before God empty-handed.

I always enjoyed giving to God with thanksgiving even though I had little, and soon I received financial blessings. I could give with joy because I knew God would give me pressed down, shaken together, and running over and even 30, 60, or 100 times more when I gave for God's kingdom with faith.

As a result, I paid back the great amount of debt that I had gained while having been in the sick-bed for seven years, and until now, I am so blessed that I do not lack anything.

Also, because I knew the law of justice that God gives His power to those who are free of evil and are sanctified, I kept on casting away evil from me through fervent prayers and fasting, and eventually I received God's power.

Today's amazing power of God is manifested because I achieved the dimension of love and justice that God has required of me while going through many hardships and trials with patience. God did not just give me His power unconditionally. He has given it to me following the rules of justice exactly. That is why the enemy devil and Satan cannot object to this.

Other than these, I believed and practiced all the words in the Bible, and I experienced all the miraculous works and blessings that are written in the Bible as well.

And such works do not take place just for me. If anybody understands the rules of justice of God written in the Bible and acts according to them, he can receive the same kinds of blessings that I have received.

Two sides of justice

Usually people think justice is something fearful which accompanies punishments. Of course, according to justice fearful punishments will follow sins and evil, but reversely, this could be the key to bring blessings for us.

Justice is like the two sides of a coin. For those who are living in darkness, it is something fearful, but for those who live in the Light, it is something very good. If a robber holds a kitchen knife it might be a murder weapon but when it's held by a mother, it is a tool for preparing food that helps her cook delicious meals for the family.

Therefore, depending on to which individual the justice of God is applied, it could be very fearful or it could be something very joyous. If we understand the two sides of justice, we can also understand that justice is fulfilled with love, and the love of God is also completed with justice. Love without justice is not true love, and justice without love cannot be true justice either.

For example, what if you punished your children every time they do something wrong? Or, what if you just leave your children unpunished all the time? In either case, you will end up causing your children to go astray.

According to justice, sometimes you need to punish your children sternly for their wrongdoings, but you cannot just show them 'justice' all the time. Sometimes you need to give them another chance, and if they really turn from their ways, you have to show forgiveness and mercy with your love. But again, you cannot just show mercy and love all the time. You need to lead your children to the right way through punishment if necessary.

God tells us about limitless forgiveness in Matthew 18:22, which says, *"I do not say to you, up to seven times, but up to seventy times seven."*

At the same time, however, God says true love is sometimes accompanied by punishment. Hebrews 12:6 says, *"For those whom the Lord loves He disciplines, and He scourges every son whom He receives."* If we understand this relationship between love and justice, we will also understand that justice is made perfect within love, and as we keep on contemplating on justice, we will understand there is deep love contained in justice.

Higher dimensions of justice

Justice also has different dimensions in different heavens. Namely, as we go up in the levels of heaven, from the first heaven to the second, third, and fourth heavens, the dimension of justice also becomes more widened and deeper. Different heavens keep their orders according to the justice of each heaven.

The reason why there is difference in the dimension of justice in each heaven is because the dimension of love in each heaven is different. Love and justice cannot be separated. The deeper the dimension of love is, the deeper the dimension of justice is too.

If we read the Bible, it might seem that the justice in the Old Testament and that in the New Testament is different from each other. For example, the Old Testament says, "An eye for an eye," which is the principle of retaliation, but in the New Testament it says, "Love your enemies." The principle of retaliation was changed into the principle of forgiveness and love. Then, does this mean the will of God was changed?

No, that is not the case. God is spirit and eternally unchanging, so the heart and will of God contained in both Old and New Testaments are the same. It's just that depending on the extent to which people have accomplished love, the same justice will be applied in different measure. Until Jesus came to this earth and fulfilled the Law with love, the level of love that people could understand was very low.

If they were told to love even their enemies, which is a very high level of justice, they wouldn't have been able to handle it. For this reason, in the Old Testament, a lower level of the rule of justice, which was 'an eye for an eye', was applied to establish order.

However, after Jesus fulfilled the Law with love by coming to this earth and giving His life for us sinners, the level of justice that God required of us humans was lifted up.

From the example of Jesus, we've already seen the level of love going from a lower level to a level of loving even our enemies. Thus the principle of retaliation saying 'an eye for an eye' is not applicable any longer. Now, God is requiring of us the dimension of justice in which the rules of forgiveness and mercy are applied. Of course, what God really wanted, even in the Old Testament era, was forgiveness and mercy, but people at that time could not really understand it.

As explained, just as there are differences in the dimension of love and justice in the Old Testament and New Testament, the dimension of justice is different depending on the dimension of love in each heaven.

For example, seeing the woman who had been caught in the act of adultery, people who acted according to the lower level justice of the first heaven said they had to stone her right away. But Jesus, who had the highest level of justice which is the justice of the fourth heaven, said to her, *"I do not condemn you, either. Go. From now on sin no more"* (John 8:11).

Therefore, justice is in our heart, and each person feels a different dimension of justice according to the extent to which they have filled their heart with love and cultivated their heart with spirit. Sometimes, for those who possess the lower dimension of justice cannot understand the justice of those who possess a higher dimension of justice.

It's because men of flesh can never completely understand what God is doing. Only those who have cultivated their heart with love and spiritual mind can precisely understand the justice of God and apply it.

But applying higher dimension of justice does not mean it will overrule or violate the justice that is in a lower dimension. Jesus possessed the justice of the fourth heaven, but He never ignored the justice of this earth. In other words, He showed the justice of the third heaven or higher on this earth within the boundary of the rules of justice of this earth.

Likewise, we cannot violate the justice that is applied in the first heaven while we are living in this first heaven. Of course, as the dimension of our love deepens, the width and depth of justice also increase, but the basic framework is the same. And thus we have to correctly understand the rules of justice.

Faith and obedience – the basic rules of justice

So, what are the basic framework and rules of justice that we have to understand and follow to receive the answers to our prayers? There are many things including, for example, goodness and humbleness. But, the two most basic principles are faith and obedience. It is the rule of justice that we receive an answer when we believe the Word of God and obey it.

The centurion in Matthew chapter 8 had a sick servant. He was a centurion of the ruling Roman Empire, but he was humble enough to come before Jesus. Also, he had the good heart to come to Jesus in person for his sick servant.

Above all, the reason why he could receive the answer was because he had faith. Until he decided to come before Jesus, he must have heard many things about Jesus from people around him. He must have heard the news about the blind coming to see, the mute coming to speak, and many sick people being healed by Jesus.

Hearing such news the centurion trusted Jesus and came to possess the faith that he could also receive his desire for his servant if he went before Him.

When he actually met with Jesus, he made a confession of faith saying, *"Lord, I am not worthy for You to come under my roof, but just say the word, and my servant will be healed"* (Matthew 8:8). He could say what he said because he completely trusted Jesus by hearing the news about him.

For us to possess such faith, we first have to repent of not obeying the Word of God. If we disappointed God in any matter, if we did not keep a promise made before God, if we did not keep the Lord's Day holy or if we did not give proper tithes, then we have to repent of all these things.

Also, we have to repent of loving the world, not having peace with people, harboring and acting with all kinds of evil such as hot-tempers, irritation, frustration, hard-feelings, envy, jealousy, quarreling, and falsehood. When we break down these walls of sins and receive the prayer of a powerful servant of God, we can be given the faith to receive answers, and we can actually receive the answer as we have believed we would, in accordance with the rules of justice.

In addition to these things, there are many other things that we have to obey and follow to receive our answers, such as attending various worship services, not ceasing to pray, and giving to God. And for us to be able to completely obey, we have to deny ourselves completely.

Namely, we have to cast away our pride, arrogance, self-righteousness and self-assertion, all our thoughts and theories, boastful pride of life, and desire to rely on the world. When we completely humble and deny ourselves this way, we can receive the answer according to the law of justice written in Luke 17:33, which says, *"Whoever seeks to keep his life will lose it, and whoever loses his life will preserve it."*

To understand the justice of God and to obey it means to acknowledge God. Because we acknowledge God, we can follow the rules that He established. And it is faith to acknowledge God in this way, and true faith is always accompanied by deeds of obedience.

If you realize any sin while reflecting upon yourself with the Word of God, you have to repent and turn from those ways. I hope you will trust God completely and rely on Him. In doing so, I hope you will realize the rules of justice of God one by one and practice them so that you will receive answers and blessings from God who lets us reap what we sow and who pays us back according to our deeds.

Princess Jane Mpologoma (London, United Kingdom)

From half-way around the globe

I live in Birmingham. It is a very beautiful place. I am a daughter of the first president of the kingdom of Buganda, and I married a gentle, kind man in the United Kingdom and have three daughters.
Many people would want to live this kind of affluent life, but I was not very happy. I always had a thirst in my soul that could not be fulfilled with anything. For a long time I had a chronic gastrointestinal disturbance which caused me a lot of pain. I could not eat or sleep well.
I had also been tormented by a variety of diseases including a high cholesterol level, a heart disorder, and low blood pressure. Doctors warned me I could have heart-attack or a stroke.
But in August 2005, I had a turning point of my life. By some chance I met with one of the assistant pastors of Manmin Central Church who was visiting London. I received books and audio sermons from him, and they touched me very profoundly.

With her husband David

They were based on the Bible, but I could not hear such deep and inspirational messages anywhere else. My thirsting soul was satisfied, and my spiritual eyes were opened to understand the Word.

Eventually I visited South Korea. The moment I walked into Manmin Central Church my whole body was wrapped with peace. I received prayer from Rev. Jaerock Lee. It was only after I came back to the UK that I realized the love of God. The results of the endoscopy done on October 21 were normal. The cholesterol level was normal, and the blood pressure was also normal. It was the power of prayer!

This experience let me have greater faith. I had heart conditions, and I wrote to Rev. Jaerock Lee to pray for me. He prayed for me during one of the Friday all-night worship services in Manmin Central Church on November 11. I received his prayer on the Internet from half-way around the globe.

He prayed, "I command in the name of Jesus Christ, heart conditions, go away. Father God, make her healthy!"

I felt the strong work of the Holy Spirit the moment I received the prayer. I would have fallen down by the strong power hadn't my husband held me. I came to my senses after 30 seconds or so.

I took an angiography on November 16. My doctor suggested it because I had a trouble in one of the arteries of the heart. It was done with a small camera fixed on a small tube. And the result was truly amazing.

The doctor said, "I've never seen such a healthy heart in this room in several years."

Thrill ran through my whole body, because I felt the hands of God when I heard my doctor's words. Since then I decided to live a different life. I wanted to reach out to the teenagers, the neglected, and anybody who is in need of the gospel.

And God made my dream come true. I and my husband have started London Manmin Church as missionaries and we are preaching the living God.

- Extract from *Extraordinary Things* -

Chapter 5 Obedience

"
Obeying the Word of God with 'Yes' and 'Amen' is the shortcut to experiencing the works of God.
"

The complete obedience of Jesus

Jesus obeyed the justice of the first heaven

People who experience the works of God
   through obedience

Obedience is the evidence of faith

Manmin Central Church taking the lead
   in world evangelism in obedience

*"And being found in appearance as a man,
He humbled Himself by becoming obedient to the point of death,
even death on a cross."*

Philippians 2:8

The Bible shows many cases where absolutely impossible things were made possible by God the Almighty. There were such miraculous things as the sun and the moon stopping and the sea being parted as people crossed it on dry ground. Such things cannot happen according to the justice of the first heaven, but it is possible according to the justice of the third heaven or above.

In order for us to experience such works of God we have to meet the conditions. There are several conditions that have to be met and among them, obedience is very important. Obeying the Word of God the Almighty with 'Yes' and 'Amen', this is the shortcut to experiencing the works of God.

1 Samuel 15:22 says, *"Samuel said, 'Has the LORD as much delight in burnt offerings and sacrifices as in obeying the voice of the LORD? Behold, to obey is better than sacrifice, and to heed than the fat of rams.'"*

The complete obedience of Jesus

Jesus obeyed the will of God until He was crucified to save the mankind who were sinners. We can be saved by faith through such obedience of Jesus. In order to understand how we can be saved by our faith in Jesus, we first have to consider how mankind went the way of death in the first place.

Before he became a sinner, Adam could have enjoyed eternal life in the Garden of Eden. But since he sinned by eating from the tree that God had forbidden, according to the law of the spiritual realm that says, 'the wages of sin is death' (Romans 6:23), he had to die and fall into Hell.

But knowing Adam would disobey, even before the ages, God prepared Jesus Christ. It was to open the way of salvation within the justice of God. Jesus, being the Word that became flesh, was born on this earth in a human body.

Because God made prophecies about the Savior, the Messiah, the enemy devil and Satan knew about the Savior, too. The devil was always looking for a chance to kill the Savior. When the three magi said Jesus had been born, the devil instigated King Herod to kill all baby boys under the age of two.

Also, the devil incited wicked people to crucify Jesus. The devil thought if he could just kill Jesus, who had come down to become the Savior, then he would lead all sinners into Hell and have all of them under his control forever.

Since Jesus had neither original sin nor self-committed sins He was not subject to be put to death according to the law of justice that says the wages of sin is death. Nonetheless, the devil, in effect, led in the killing of Jesus and thereby violated the law of justice.

As a result, sinless Jesus overcame death and resurrected. And now, anyone who believes in Jesus Christ can be saved and gain eternal life. At first, according to the law of justice saying that the wages of sin is death, Adam and his descendants were destined to go the way of death, but later, the way of salvation was opened through Jesus Christ. This is the 'mystery hidden since before the ages' in 1 Corinthians 2:7.

Jesus never thought like, "Why should I be killed for sinners even though I have no sin?" He willingly took the cross to be crucified according to the providence of God. It was this thorough and complete obedience of Jesus that opened the pathway for our salvation.

Jesus obeyed the justice of the first heaven

During His entire life on this earth, Jesus obeyed the will of God thoroughly and lived according to the law of the justice of the first heaven. Though He was God in the very nature, He put on a human body and He experienced hunger, tiredness, pain, sorrow, and loneliness just like men.

Before He began His public ministry He fasted for 40 days. And though He is the master of all things, He fervently cried out in prayer and prayed continually. He was tested by the devil three times towards the end of His 40-day fast, and He drove away the devil with the Word of God, without being tempted or swayed at all.

Also, Jesus has the power of God, so He could manifest any kind of miracle and amazing things. And yet, He showed such miracles only when they were necessary according to the providence of God. He showed the power of the Son of God by such events as making wine from water and feeding 5,000 men with five loaves and two fish.

Had He desired it, He could have destroyed those who ridiculed and crucified Him. But, He quietly received the persecution and scorn and in obedience, He was crucified. He felt all the sufferings and pains as a man and He shed all His blood and water.

Hebrews 5:8-9 says, *"Although He was a Son, He learned obedience from the things which He suffered. And having been made perfect, He became to all those who obey Him the source of eternal salvation."*

Because Jesus fulfilled the law of justice through His complete obedience, anyone who accepts the Lord Jesus and lives in the truth can become a servant of righteousness and reach salvation without having to go the way of death as servants of sin (Romans 6:16).

People who experience the works of God through obedience

Though He is the Son of God, Jesus fulfilled the providence of God because He completely obeyed. Then, how much more should we mere creatures obey completely to experience the works of God? Complete obedience is required.

In John chapter 2, Jesus performed a miracle by changing water into wine. When they ran out of wine at a banquet, the Virgin Mary specifically instructed the servants to do whatever Jesus would tell them to do. Jesus told the servants to 'fill water pots and then to draw the water and take it to the master of the feast'. When the master of the feast tasted the water, the water had already been made good wine.

If the servants had not obeyed Jesus telling them to take the water to the master of the feast, they could not have experienced the miracle of wine. Knowing the law of obedience and justice very well, the Virgin Mary requested that the servants be sure to obey Him.

We can also consider Peter's obedience. Peter had not caught any fish all night. But, when Jesus commanded, "Put out into the deep and let down your nets for a catch", Peter obeyed saying, *"Master, we worked hard all night and caught nothing, but I will do as You say and let down the nets."* Then, they enclosed a great quantity of fish, and their nets began to break (Luke 5:4-6).

Because Jesus, who was one with God the Creator, spoke with the original voice, a large number of fish obeyed His command immediately and went into the net. But, if Peter had not obeyed Jesus' command, what would have happened? If he had said, "Sir, I know about catching fish better than you. We tried to catch fish all night and now we are very tired. We're done for today. It will surely be tiresome to put down into the deep and let the net down" then, no miracle would have occurred.

A widow in Zarephath in 1 Kings chapter 17 also experienced the work of God through her obedience. After a long drought her food was running out and there remained only a handful of flour and a little oil. One day Elijah came to her and asked for the food, saying, *"For thus says the LORD God of Israel, 'The bowl of flour shall not be exhausted, nor shall the jar of oil be empty, until the day that the LORD sends rain on the face of the earth'"* (1 Kings 17:14).

The widow and her son would have to wait for the day they would die after eating the last bit of food. However, she believed and obeyed the Word of God delivered to her by Elijah. She gave all her food to Elijah. Now, God performed a miracle for the obedient woman as He promised. The bowl of flour was not used up and the jar of oil did not run dry until the serious drought ended. The widow, her son, and Elijah were saved.

Obedience is the evidence of faith

Mark 9:23 says, *"And Jesus said to him, '"If You can?" All things are possible to him who believes.'"*

This is the law of justice saying that if we believe, then we can experience the works of the almighty God. If we pray with faith, then sicknesses will leave and if we command with faith, then demons will go out and all kinds of hardships and trials will go away. If we pray with faith, we can receive financial blessings. All things are possible with faith!

It is the deed of obedience that testifies that we have the faith to receive answers according to the law of justice. James 2:22 says, *"You see that faith was working with his works, and as a result of the works, faith was perfected."* James 2:26 says, *"For just as the body without the spirit is dead, so also faith without works is dead."*

Elijah asked the widow of Zarephath to bring her last food for him. If she had said, "I believe you are a man of God and I believe God will bless me and my food will never run out," but had not obeyed, then she would not have experienced any work of God. That's because her deeds would not have shown the evidence of her faith.

But the widow trusted in Elijah's words. As the evidence of her faith, she brought him the last of her food, obeying his words. This deed of obedience testified to her faith, and a miracle took place according to the law of justice, which says all things are possible to him who believes.

To achieve visions and dreams given by God, our faith and obedience is very important. Patriarchs such as Abraham, Jacob, and Joseph put the Word of God in their mind and obeyed.

When Joseph was young, God gave him the dream of becoming an honorable man. Joseph did not only believe the dream but he also remembered it all the time and he did not change his mind until he accomplished the dream. He looked up to the work of God in any circumstances and followed God's guidance.

Being a slave and a prisoner for 13 years, he did not doubt the dream God had given him, although the reality looked like the opposite of his dreams. He just walked the right way obeying the commandments of God. God saw his faith and obedience and fulfilled his dream. All trials came to an end, and at the age of 30 he became the second most powerful man in the whole country of Egypt next only to the Pharaoh, the king.

Manmin Central Church, taking the lead in world evangelism in obedience

Today Manmin Central Church has more than ten thousand branch/associative churches around the world and is preaching the gospel to every corner of the world via Internet service, satellite TV, and other media. The church has shown the deeds of obedience in accordance with the law of justice from the beginning of all these ministries until today.

Since the moment I met God, all my diseases were healed, and my dream was to become a proper elder in the sight of God who would glorify God and help many poor people. But one day God called me as His servant saying, "I selected you as My servant before the ages." And He said that if I had equipped myself with the Word of God for three years, I would cross the oceans, rivers and mountains and perform miraculous signs wherever I would go.

In reality, I was still a relatively new believer. I was introversive and poor at speaking before a crowd. However, I obeyed it without any excuse and became a servant of God. I did my best to walk according to the Word of God in the 66 books of the Bible and I prayed with fasting in the guidance of the Holy Spirit. I have obeyed just as the way God commanded.

When I had mega size overseas crusades, I did not plan or prepare for them in my way, but only obeyed the command of God. I went only where He commanded me to go. For mega size crusades, it would usually take years to prepare, but if God commanded, we prepared for them in just a few months.

Even though we did not have enough money to hold those mega size crusades, if we prayed, then God fulfilled our finances every time. Sometimes God commanded me to go to those countries where preaching gospel was not actually possible.

In 2002, while we were preparing a crusade in Chennai, India, the Tamil Nadu government announced the new ordinance banning forcible conversions. The ordinance regulated that no person should convert or attempt to convert any person from one religion to another by the use of force or by allurement or any fraudulent means. Contravention could bring about a jail term up to five years and a fine, if the convert is "a minor, a woman or a person belonging to a Scheduled Caste or Scheduled Tribe". The fine of Rs.1 lakh is 100,000 rupees that is two thousand day's worth of wage.

Our crusade at the Marina Beach aimed at not only Indian

Christians but also many Hindus, who make up more than 80 % of the whole population.

The Ordinance of the Prohibition of Forcible Conversion was supposed to be enacted beginning the first day of our crusade. So, I had to feel ready for jail when I preached the gospel on the stage of the crusade. Some people told me that the Tamil Nadu police would come and watch our crusade to record my preaching.

In this threatening situation, Indian ministers and the organizing committee felt strained and tense. But I took courage and obeyed God because God had commanded it. I was not afraid of being arrested or going to jail, and courageously proclaimed God the Creator and the Savior Jesus Christ.

Then, God conducted amazing things. While preaching, I spoke, "If you come to have faith in your heart, stand up and walk." At that moment, a boy began to get up and walk. The boy, before he attended the crusade, had his pelvis and a hip joint cut during an operation and had the two parts linked with a metal plate. He suffered from severe pain after the operation and could not walk a step without crutches. But when I commanded, "Stand up and walk," he immediately threw away the crutches and began to walk.

That day, in addition to this miracle of the teenage boy, a lot of amazing works of the power of God took place. The blind came to see, the deaf to hear, and the mute to speak. They stood up from their wheelchairs and threw away their crutches. The news quickly spread to the city and many more people gathered the next day.

A total of three million people attended the meetings and more surprisingly, more than 60% of those in attendance were Hindus. They had Hindu marks on their foreheads. After they listened to the message and witnessed God's powerful works, they took off the marks and determined to convert to Christianity.

The crusade brought about union of the local Christians, and eventually the ordinance against forcible conversions was abolished. Such a wonderful work was done through the obedience to the Word of God. Now, in order to experience such amazing works of God, what specifically do we have to obey?

First, we have to obey the 66 books of the Bible.

We should not obey the Word of God only when God Himself appears before us and tells us something. We have to obey the words that are written in the 66 books of the Bible all the time. We should understand the will of God and obey it through the Bible, and then we can obey the messages that are preached in the church. Namely, the words that tell us to do, not do, keep, or cast away certain things are the rules of justice of God, and thus, we should obey them.

For example, you hear that you have to repent of your sins and with tears and runny noses. It is the law that says we can receive an answer from God only after we demolish the wall of sin standing between God and us (Isaiah 59:1-2). Also, you hear that you have to cry out in prayer. It is the method of prayer that brings down answers according to the law that dictates we eat the fruit of our sweat and toil (Luke 22:44).

In order to meet God and receive His answers, we first have to repent of our sins and cry out in our prayer asking God what we need. If anybody demolishes his wall of sin, prays with all his strength, and shows his deeds of faith, he can meet God and receive answers. This is a law of justice.

Second, we have to believe and obey the words of the servants of God whom God is with.

Right after the opening of the church, a cancer patient was carried to the church on a stretcher to attend the worship service. I told him to sit up to attend the service. His wife supported him from the back and he could barely sit during the worship service. Would I not have known that it was very difficult for him to sit up since he was very ill and had to be carried on a stretcher? But I gave him the advice by the inspiration of the Holy Spirit, and he obeyed.

Seeing his obedience, God immediately granted him divine healing. Namely, all his pains were gone and he could stand and walk by himself.

Just as a widow of Zarephath had obeyed the word of Elijah by trusting a man of God, that man's obedience became the way to God's answer for him. He could not be healed with his own faith. But he experienced the healing power of God because he obeyed the word of a man of God who performed God's power.

Third, we have to obey the works of the Holy Spirit.

Next, in order to receive the answers from God, we should instantly follow the voice of the Holy Spirit given while we are praying and listening to the sermons. That's because the Holy Spirit dwelling in us leads us to the way of blessings and answers according to the law of justice.

For example, during the sermon, if the Holy Spirit urges you to pray more after the service, you can just obey. If you obey, you may be able to repent of your sins that have not been forgiven for a long time or receive the gift of tongue in the grace of God. Sometimes, some blessings come during your prayers.

When I was a new believer, I had to do hard labor on construction sites to make ends meet. I walked home with such a tired body just to save the bus fare. But if the Holy Spirit moved my heart to offer a certain amount of church construction offering or thanks-giving offering, I just obeyed.

I gave without using my own thoughts. If I had no money, I made a vow to give to God by a certain date. And I got the money with all my efforts by the appointed date and gave it to God. As I obeyed, God blessed me more and more with the things that He had prepared.

God sees our obedience and opens the door of answers and blessings. For me personally, He has given me various answers big and small to whatever I asked, and not only financial things. He has given me anything I asked if I just obeyed Him with faith.

2 Corinthians 1:19-20 says, *"For the Son of God, Christ Jesus, who was preached among you by us--by me and Silvanus and Timothy--was not yes and no, but is yes in Him. For as many as are the promises of God, in Him they are yes; therefore also through Him is our Amen to the glory of God through us."*

In order for us to experience the works of God according to the law of justice, we have to show the deeds of faith through our obedience. Just as Jesus set an example, if we just obey regardless of our circumstances or conditions, then God's works will be unfolded before us greatly. I hope you will all obey God's Word with only 'Yes' and 'Amen' and experience the works of God in your daily lives.

Dr. Paul Ravindran Ponraj (Chennai, India)
- Senior House Officer, Cardio-thoracic Surgery at Southampton General Hospital, UK
- Registrar Cardio-thoracic Surgery at St. Georges Hospital, London, U.K.
- Senior Registrar Cardiothoracic Surgery, HAREFIELD Hospital, Middlesex, U.K.
- Cardiothoracic Surgeon, Willingdon Hospital, Chennai

Power of God beyond medicine

I have used the handkerchief carrying the anointing on many sick patients and have seen them recover. I always keep the handkerchief in my shirt pocket when I am in the operating room doing surgery. I would like to recount a miracle that took place in 2005.

A young man aged 42; a building contractor by profession from one of the towns in Tamil Nadu state came to me with coronary artery disease and was required to undergo coronary artery bypass surgery. I had prepared him for surgery and he was operated on. It was a very simple straight forward 2 bypass graft surgery (off pump) performed with the heart beating. The surgery was over in about two and a half hours.

As his chest was being closed he became unstable with abnormal ECG and drop in blood pressure. I reopened his chest and found that the bypass grafts were perfect. He was shifted to the catheterization lab to do an angiogram check. It was found that all his blood vessels in the heart and the large blood vessels in his leg had gone into spasm with no blood flowing. The reason for this we have not been able to ascertain even today.

There was no hope for this young man. He was taken to the operating room with external heart massage and chest was opened again and the heart was massaged directly for over 20 minutes. He was connected to the heart lung machine.

A variety of vasodilator drugs were given to relieve the spasm but there was no response. He was maintaining a mean blood pressure on pump of 25 to 30 mmHg. for over 7 hours and I was aware that blood supply and oxygen at that pressure was inadequate for his brain to function.

At the end of 18 hours of struggle and 7 hours of heart on pump with no positive response, we decided to close the chest and declare the patient dead. I went on my knees and prayed. I said, "God if that is what you want it to be so be it." I have started the surgery with prayer and have all along carried the anointed handkerchief given by Dr. Jaerock Lee in my pocket, and I recalled what has been said in

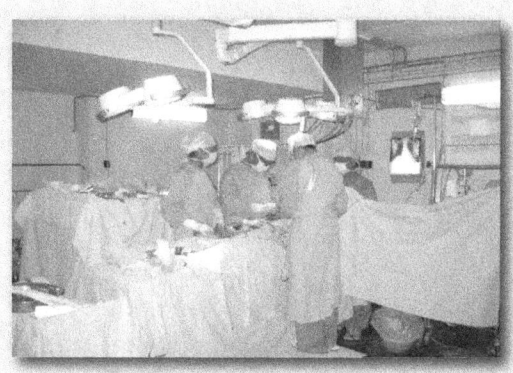

Dr. Paul Ponraj performing surgery (center)

Acts 19:12. I got up from prayer and walked into the operating room as the chest was being closed before declaring the patient dead.
A sudden change occurred and the patient became absolutely normal. The ECG became totally normal. The entire team was shocked and one member of the team, a non-believer said the God you had faith in has honored you. Yes, it is true when you walk in faith you are in the middle of a miracle and at the end of disaster. This young man walked out of the hospital with no neurological deficit except for a little swelling in his right leg. He testified in a prayer cell that he was going to do God's work as he has received a second life.

- Extract from *Extraordinary Things* -

Chapter 6 Faith

> If we have full assurance of faith,
> we can bring down the power of God
> even in the face of seemingly impossible situations.

A sincere heart and full assurance of faith

The relationship between faith and sincerity

Ask in full assurance of faith

Abraham with sincere heart in full assurance of faith

To cultivate a sincere heart and full assurance of faith

Tests of faith

Pakistan crusade

*"... let us draw near with a sincere heart
in full assurance of faith,
having our hearts sprinkled clean from an evil conscience
and our bodies washed with pure water."*

Hebrews 10:22

People receive answers from God in different measures. Some receive the answer just by praying for it once or just by desiring it in their heart while others have to offer many days of prayers and fasting. For some people, they perform signs, controlling the power of darkness and healing the sick through the prayer of faith (Mark 16:17-18). On the contrary, some people say they pray with faith, but there are no signs or wonders taking place through their prayers.

If anyone suffers from a disease even though he is a believer in God and he is praying, he needs to reflect on his faith. The words in the Bible are the truth that never change eternally, and thus if anyone has the faith that can be recognized by God, he can receive anything he asks for. Jesus promised us in Matthew 21:22, *"And all things you ask in prayer, believing, you will receive."* Now, what is the reason that people receive the answer from God in different measures?

A sincere heart and full assurance of faith

Hebrews 10:22 says, *"... let us draw near with a sincere heart in full assurance of faith, having our hearts sprinkled clean from an evil conscience and our bodies washed with pure water."* The sincere heart here stands for the true heart that has no falsehood. It is the heart that resembles the heart of Jesus Christ.

Simply put, full assurance of faith is perfect faith. It is to believe all the words of the 66 books of the Bible without any doubt and to keep all the commandments of God. To the extent that we possess a sincere heart we can have perfect faith. The confession of those who have accomplished a true heart is the true confession of faith. God answers the prayer of these people quickly.

Many people confess their faith before God, but the sincerity in their confessions is all different. There are people whose confessions of faith are 100% true because their heart is 100% sincere, while there are some others whose confessions of faith are only 50% true because their heart is only 50% sincere. If one's heart is only 50% sincere, God will say, "You only trust me half way." *The sincerity contained in one's confession of faith is one's measure of faith that is acknowledged by God.*

The relationship between faith and sincerity

In our relationships with others, saying that we trust the other person and the actual extent to which we trust that person may be quite different. For example, when mothers go outside leaving their young children at home, what do they say? They might say, "You should behave yourselves and stay in the house. Children, I am trusting you." Now, does the mother really trust her children?

If a mother truly trusts her child, she doesn't have to say, "I trust you." She can just say, "I will be back by so and so time." But she adds a little bit more when her child is not trustworthy. She might add, "I just cleaned up, so keep the house neat. Do not touch my cosmetics, and you should not turn on the gas burner." She goes over each point with which she is not comfortable and before she goes out she tells her child, "I am trusting you, so listen to my words..."

If the amount of trust were even less, even after she told her child what to do, she may call home and check what her child is doing. She asks, "What are you doing now? Is everything OK?" and tries to find out what her child is doing. She said she trusted her child but in her heart she can't trust fully. The measure of parents' trust in their children is all different.

You can trust some children more than other children according to how sincere and trustworthy they actually are. If they listen to their parents all the time, their parents can trust them 100%. When these parents say, "I trust you," this is really true.

Ask in full assurance of faith

Now, if a child, whom his parents trust 100%, asks for something, the parents might just give the child what he asks for. They don't have to ask him, "What are you going to do with it?" "Do you really need it now?" and so on. They can just give him what he wants in full trust thinking, 'He asks for it because it is definitely necessary. He will not waste anything.'

But if the parents do not have the full measure of trust, they will comply only when they can understand the proper reason for their child's request. The less trust they have, the less they can believe what their child says and they hesitate to grant the child what he asks for. If the child keeps on asking again and again, the parents sometimes just give it to him, not because they believe him, but only because their child asks them so much.

This principle works in the same way between God and us. Do you have the sincere heart so that God can acknowledge your faith 100%, saying, "My son, my daughter, you believe Me in full assurance?"

We shouldn't be the ones who receive from God only because we ask so much day and night. We should be able to receive whatever we ask by walking in the truth in all things, having nothing by which we can be condemned (1 John 3:21-22).

Abraham with sincere heart in full assurance of faith

The reason why Abraham could become the father of faith is because he had true heart and full assurance of faith. Abraham believed in God's promise and never doubted it in any situation.

God promised Abraham, when he was 75 years old, that a great nation would be formed through him. But for more than next 20 years from that time, he did not get any child. When he was 99 and his wife Sarah 89, when they were too old to have any child, God said they would have a son after a year. Romans 4:19-22 explains the situation.

It says, *"Without becoming weak in faith he contemplated his own body, now as good as dead since he was about a hundred years old, and the deadness of Sarah's womb; yet, with respect to the promise of God, he did not waver in unbelief but grew strong in faith, giving glory to God, and being fully assured that what God had promised, He was able also to perform. Therefore it was also credited to him as righteousness."*

Although it was something absolutely impossible with human ability, Abraham never doubted but believed in the promise of God fully, and God acknowledged Abraham's faith. God let him have a son, Isaac, the next year, as He promised.

But for Abraham to become the father of faith, there was another test remaining. Abraham had Isaac at the age of 100, and Isaac grew up well. Abraham loved his son very much. At this time, God commanded Abraham to offer Isaac as a burnt offering the way they gave cows or lambs as burnt offerings. During the Old Testament times they removed the skin, cut the animal into pieces, and then gave it as a burnt offering.

Hebrews 11:17-19 well explains how Abraham acted at this moment, *"By faith Abraham, when he was tested, offered up Isaac, and he who had received the promises was in the act of offering up his only son, of whom it was said, "Through Isaac shall your offspring be named." He considered that God was able even to raise him from the dead, from which, figuratively speaking, he did receive him back"* (Hebrews 11:17-19 ESVUK).

Abraham tied Isaac on the altar, and was just about to cut his son with a knife. At that moment, an angel from God appeared and said, *"Do not stretch out your hand against the lad, and do nothing to him; for now I know that you fear God, since you have not withheld your son, your only son, from Me"* (Genesis 22:12). Through this test, Abraham's perfect faith was acknowledged by God and he proved himself qualified to become the Father of Faith.

To cultivate the sincere heart and full assurance of faith

I once had a time when I had no hope and I only waited for death. But my sister took me to a church and just by kneeling down in a sanctuary of God I was healed of all my diseases by the power of God. It was the answer for my sister's prayers and fasting for me.

Since I received overwhelming love and grace from God, I wanted to know about Him so much. I attended many revival meetings on top of all kinds of worship services to learn the Word of God. Although I was doing physically demanding work on a construction site, I attended dawn prayer meetings every morning. I just wanted to hear the Word of God and learn His will the best I could.

When the pastors taught the will of God, I just obeyed it. I heard it was not right for a child of God to smoke and drink, so I immediately quit smoking and drinking. Since I heard we had to give God our tithes and offerings, I have never missed giving them to God until this day.

As I read the Bible, I did what God tells us to do and kept what God tells us to keep. I did not do what the Bible says not to do. I prayed, and even fasted to cast off the things that the Bible tells us to throw away. If it was not easy to cast them away, I fasted to do it. God considered my effort to pay back God's grace and gave me precious faith.

My faith in God became increasingly firmer day after day. I never doubted God in any test or hardship. As a result of obeying God's Word, my heart was changing into a sincere heart that has no falsehood. It was changing into a good and pure heart to become more like the heart of the Lord.

As said in 1 John 3:21, *"Beloved, if our heart does not condemn us, we have confidence before God;"* I asked God anything with confident faith, and I received the answers.

Tests of faith

Meanwhile, in February 1983, 7 months after opening of the church, there was a great test of my faith. My three daughters and a young man were found poisoned by carbon monoxide gas early one Saturday morning. It was right after the Friday all-night worship service. It did not seem possible for them to live again because they had inhaled the gas for almost the whole night.

Their eyeballs were turned and they had bubbles in their mouths. Their bodies did not have any strength and were dangling. I had the church members lay them on the floor of the sanctuary, went up to the altar, and offered God a prayer of thanks.

"Father God, thank You. You gave and You took them away. I thank You for taking my daughters to the bosom of the Lord. I thank You, God, for taking them to Your kingdom where there are no tears, sorrow, or pain."

"But since the young man is a just member of the church, I ask You to revive him. I do not want this incident to disgrace Your name..."

After praying to God in this way, I first prayed for the young man, and then for my three daughters one after the other. Then, not even a couple of minutes after I prayed for them, the four of them all stood up in clear consciousness in the order I had prayed for them.

Because I truly trusted and loved God, I offered up prayer of thanksgiving without holding any grudges or sorrow in my heart, and God was moved by this prayer and showed us a great miracle. Our members could have greater faith through this incident. My faith was also recognized by God more greatly and I received greater power from God. Namely, I learned how to drive away poisonous gas, even though it is not a living organism.

When there is a test of faith, if we show our unchanging faith to God, God will acknowledge our faith and reward us with blessings. Even the enemy devil and Satan cannot accuse us anymore because they also saw that our faith is true faith.

From that time on I could overcome all trials, always drawing nearer to God with a sincere heart and perfect faith. Each time, I received greater power from above. With the power of God given to me in this way, God let me have overseas united crusades beginning in the year 2000.

While I was offering up a 40-day fast in 1982, before the opening of the church, God accepted it joyfully and gave me the missions of World Evangelism and Building the Grand Sanctuary. Even after five years or ten years, I could not see any way to accomplish those missions. Yet, I still believed God would fulfill them and prayed for these missions continually.

Over the next 17 years from the opening of the church, God blessed us to accomplish world evangelism through mega size overseas crusades where the amazing power of God was manifested. Beginning with Uganda, we also had united crusades in Japan, Pakistan, Kenya, Philippines, India, Dubai, Russia, Germany, Peru, DR Congo, the United States, and even Israel, where gospel preaching is practically impossible. And there were tremendous healing works that took place. Many people converted from Hinduism and Islam. We gave glory to God greatly.

When the time came, God let us publish many books in various languages to preach the gospel through publications. He also let us establish a Christian TV channel called Global Christian Network (GCN), and a network of Christian medical doctors, World Christian Doctors Network (WCDN), all to spread the works of God's power manifested in our church.

Pakistan crusade

There were many occasions that we overcame with faith in overseas crusades, but I would like to talk about the Pakistan crusade in particular that was held in October, 2000.

On the day of the united crusade, we had a ministers' conference. Though we had already received approval from the government, the conference location was closed down when we went there in the morning. The majority of the population of Pakistan is Muslim. There were threats of terrorism against our Christian meeting. Since our meeting was well publicized by the media, the Muslims tried to disturb our crusade.

That is why the government changed their attitude so suddenly, cancelled the permission to use the venue, and blocked the people who were coming to attend the conference. However, I was not disturbed or even surprised in my mind. Rather, as my heart was moved, I said, "The conference will begin by noon today." I confessed my faith while the armed policemen were blocking the gates and there seemed to be no chance of the government officials changing their minds.

God foreknew things would go this way and prepared the minister of culture and sports of the Pakistani government who could solve this problem. He was in Lahore for business, and while he was going to the airport to go back to Islamabad, he heard about our situation and called the police department and state government officials, so that the meeting could be held. He even delayed the departure of his flight so he could come and visit the location where the conference was being held.

By the amazing work of God the gate of the ground opened, and so many people rushed in with cheers and shouts of joy. They hugged one another and shed tears out of their deep emotion and joy, giving glory to God. And, it was exactly at noon!

The next day, in the crusade, great works of God's power were manifested in the midst of the greatest number of people in the Christian history of Pakistan. It also opened a way for a missionary work in the Middle East. Since then, we gave glory to God greatly in each country we went for a crusade having the greatest crowds and the most powerful works of God.

Just as we can open any door if we have the "master key," if we have perfect faith, we can bring down the power of God in the face of the most impossible of situations. Then, all problems can be solved in a moment.

Also, even though accidents, natural disasters, or contagious diseases are prevailing, we can be protected by God if only we draw near to God with sincere hearts and perfect faith. Also, even if people with authority or those who are evil try to bring you down with schemes, if you just have a true heart and perfect faith, you will be able to give glory to God like Daniel who was protected in the lion's den.

The first part of 2 Chronicles 16:9 says, *"For the eyes of the LORD move to and fro throughout the earth that He may strongly support those whose heart is completely His."* Even the children of God will face many kinds of small and big problems in their lives. At those times, God expects them to rely on Him, praying with perfect faith.

Those who come to God with true heart will repent of their sins thoroughly when their sins are revealed. Once their sins are forgiven, they gain confidence, and they can go near to God with full assurance of faith (Hebrews 10:22). I pray in the name of the Lord that you will understand this principle and go near to God with sincere heart and perfect faith, so that you will receive the answers to whatever you ask in prayer.

Third heaven and
space of the third dimension

The third heaven is where the kingdom of heaven is located.
The space that has the characteristics of the third heaven is called the 'space of the third dimension'.

When it's hot and humid in summer, we say it's like a tropical area. This does not mean the hot and humid air in the tropical area actually moved to that place.
It's just that the weather there has the similar characteristics of the weather in tropical areas.
In the same way, even if things of the third heaven take place in the first heaven (the physical space we live in), it does not mean a particular part of the space of the third heaven came out to the first heaven.

Of course, when the heavenly host, angels, or prophets travel to the first heaven, the gates that connect the third heaven will be opened.
Just as astronauts have to be in a space suit for moon-walks or space-walks, when beings in the third heaven come down to the first heaven, they have to 'put on' the space of the third dimension.

Some of the patriarchs in the Bible also experienced the space of the third heaven. They are usually the occasions when angels or angels of the LORD appeared and helped them.

Peter and Paul set free from jail

Acts 12:7-10 says, *"And behold, an angel of the Lord suddenly appeared and a light shone in the cell; and he struck Peter's side and woke him up, saying, "Get up quickly." And his chains fell off his hands. And the angel said to him, "Gird yourself and put on your sandals." And he did so. And he said to him, "Wrap your cloak around you and follow me." And he went out and continued to follow, and he did not know that what was being done by the angel was real, but thought he was seeing a vision. When they had passed the first and second guard, they came to the iron gate that leads into the city, which opened for them by itself; and they went out and went along one street, and immediately the angel departed from him."*

Acts 16:25-26 says, *"But about midnight Paul and Silas were praying and singing hymns of praise to God, and the prisoners were listening to them; and suddenly there came a great earthquake, so that the foundations of the prison house were shaken; and immediately all the doors were opened and everyone's chains were unfastened."*

These were the events when Peter and the apostle Paul were put in jail without any fault, only because they were preaching the gospel. They were persecuted while preaching the gospel, but they did not complain at all. But they rather praised God and rejoiced over the fact that they could suffer for the name of the Lord. Because their hearts were proper according to the justice of the third heaven, God sent angels to them to set them free. The fastened stocks or gates of iron were not a problem for the angels.

Daniel survived lions' den

When Daniel was a prime minister of the Persian Empire, some of those who were jealous of him schemed to destroy him. Consequently he was thrown into a lions' den. But Daniel 6:22 says, *"My God sent His angel and shut the lions' mouths and they have not harmed me, inasmuch as I was found innocent before Him; and also toward you, O king, I have committed no crime."* Here, 'God sent His angel and shut the lions' mouths' means that the space of the third heaven covered them.

In the kingdom of heaven in the third heaven, even animals that are ferocious on earth, like lions, are not violent but very mild. So, the actual lions of this earth also became very mild when the space of the third heaven covered them. But if that space is lifted, they will go back to their original violent characters. Daniel 6:24 says, *"The king then gave orders, and they brought those men who had maliciously accused Daniel, and they cast them, their children and their wives into the lions' den; and they had not reached the bottom of the den before the lions overpowered them and crushed all their bones."*

Daniel was protected by God because he had not sinned at all. The evil people tried to find grounds to accuse him, but they couldn't find any. Also, he prayed even though his life was threatened. All his acts were proper according to the justice of the third dimension, and for this reason a space of the third dimension covered the lions' den and Daniel was not hurt at all.

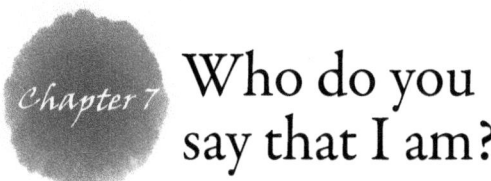

Chapter 7 Who do you say that I am?

> "You are the Christ, the Son of the living God."
> If you make confession of faith
> from the depth of your heart,
> it will be followed by your deeds.
> God blesses those who make such a confession.

Importance of confession of the lips

Peter walked on water

Peter received keys of heaven

The reason why Peter received amazing blessing

Practice the Word if you believe Jesus as your Savior

To receive answers before Jesus

Receiving answers through the confession of lips

He said to them, "But who do you say that I am?"
Simon Peter answered, "You are the Christ, the Son of the living God."
And Jesus said to him, "Blessed are you, Simon Barjona,
because flesh and blood did not reveal this to you,
but My Father who is in heaven. "I also say to you that you are Peter,
and upon this rock I will build My church;
and the gates of Hades will not overpower it.
"I will give you the keys of the kingdom of heaven;
and whatever you bind on earth shall have been bound in heaven,
and whatever you loose on earth shall have been loosed in heaven."

Matthew 16:15-19

Some married couples rarely say "I love you," for their whole marriage life. If we ask them, they could say the heart is important, and they don't really have to say it all the time. Of course, the heart is more important than merely confessing with the lips.

No matter how many times we say "I love you," if we do not love from our heart, the words are useless. But would it not be better if we could confess what we have in our heart? Spiritually, it is the same.

Importance of confession of the lips

Romans 10:10 says, *"...for with the heart a person believes, resulting in righteousness, and with the mouth he confesses, resulting in salvation."*

Of course, what this verse emphasizes is to believe with our heart. We cannot be saved just by confessing with our lips, "I believe," but by believing from the heart. However, it still says we have to confess with our lips what we believe in our heart. Why?

It is to tell us the importance of the actions that follow the confession of lips. Those who confess that they believe, but do so only with their lips without having faith in their hearts, cannot show the evidence of their faith, which are their actions or deeds of faith.

But those who truly believe in heart and confess it with their lips show the evidences of their faith with their actions. Namely, they do what God says to do, do not do what God tells us not to do, keep what God tells us to keep, and they throw away what God tells us to throw away.

That is why James 2:22 says, *"You see that faith was working with his works, and as a result of the works, faith was perfected."* Matthew 7:21 also says, *"Not everyone who says to Me, 'Lord, Lord,' will enter the kingdom of heaven, but he who does the will of My Father who is in heaven will enter."* Namely, it is shown that we can be saved only when we follow the will of God.

If you make a confession of faith that comes from the heart, it will be accompanied by deeds. Then, God considers this true faith and will answer and lead you to the way of blessings. In Matthew 16:15-19, we see Peter received such an amazing blessing through his confession of faith that came out from the depths of his heart.

Jesus asked the disciples, *"Who do you say that I am?"* Peter answered, *"You are the Christ, the Son of the living God."* How could he make such a marvelous confession of faith?

In Matthew 14, we read about the situation where Peter made a remarkable confession of faith. It is when Peter walked on the water. For a man to be walking on water does not make any sense by human knowledge. Jesus walking on water is amazing by itself, and also it draws fast our attention when Peter walked on the water, too.

Peter walked on water

At that time, Jesus had been praying alone in the mountains, and in the middle of the night, He approached His disciples who were on a boat, battered by the waves. The disciples thought He was a ghost. Just imagine a being at dark night approaching you in the middle of the sea! The disciples cried out of fear.

Jesus, said, *"Take courage, it is I; do not be afraid."* And Peter replied, *"Lord, if it is You, command me to come to You on the water."* Jesus said, *"Come!"* and then Peter got out of the boat, walked on the water and came toward Jesus.

Peter could walk on the water but it was not because his faith was perfect. We can understand this from the fact that he was afraid and began to sink when he saw the wind. Jesus reached out and caught him and said, "You of little faith, why did you doubt?" If not by perfect faith, then how was it that Peter was able to walk on the water?

Although it could not be done with his own faith, he believed Jesus, the Son of God, in his heart and acknowledged Him so that he could walk on the water for that moment. At this point, we can realize something very important: it is important to confess with lips when we believe in the Lord and acknowledge Him.

Before Peter walked on water, he confessed, *"Lord, if it is You, command me to come to You on the water."* Of course, we cannot say this confession was a complete one. If he had believed in the Lord in his heart 100%, he would have confessed, "Lord, you can do anything. Tell me to come to you on the water."

But, since Peter did not have enough faith to make a perfect confession from the depth of his heart, he said, *"Lord, if it is You."* He was somewhat asking for confirmation. Still, Peter was differentiated from other disciples on the boat by saying this.

He made a confession of his faith as soon as he recognized Jesus while the other disciples were crying out of fear. When Peter believed and acknowledged Jesus and confessed Him as the Lord from the depth of his heart, he could experience such a miraculous thing that couldn't be done by his own faith and power, which was to walk on the water.

Peter received keys of heaven

Through the above experience, Peter eventually made a perfect confession of his faith. In Matthew 16:16, Peter said, *"You are the Christ, the Son of the living God."* This was a different kind of confession from the one he made at the time of walking on the water. During Jesus' ministry, not everybody believed and recognized Him as the Messiah. Some were envious of Him and tried to kill Him.

There were even people who judged and condemned Him making false rumors such as 'He was crazy', 'He was possessed by Beelzebub', or 'As the prince of demons He was driving out demons'.

Still, in Matthew 16:13, Jesus asks His disciples, *"Who do people say that the Son of Man is?"* They replied, *"Some say John the Baptist; and others, Elijah; but still others, Jeremiah, or one of the prophets."* There were also bad rumors about Jesus, but the disciples did not mention them but only talked about good things so that they might encourage Jesus.

Now Jesus asked them again, *"Who do you say that I am?"* The first one who answered this question was Peter. He said in Matthew 16:16, *"You are the Christ, the Son of the living God."* We read in the following verses that Jesus gave Peter such a blessed word.

"Blessed are you, Simon Barjona, because flesh and blood did not reveal this to you, but My Father who is in heaven" (Matthew 16:17).

"I also say to you that you are Peter, and upon this rock I will build My church; and the gates of Hades will not overpower it. I will give you the keys of the kingdom of heaven; and whatever you bind on earth shall have been bound in heaven, and whatever you loose on earth shall have been loosed in heaven" (Matthew 16:18-19).

Peter received the blessing of becoming the foundation of the church and the authority to show things of spiritual space in this physical space. That is how numerous wondrous things took place through Peter at later times; lame men came to walk, the dead were revived, and thousands of people repented at one time.

Also, when Peter cursed Ananias and Sapphira who cheated the Holy Spirit, they immediately fell and died (Acts 5:1-11). All these things were possible because the apostle Peter had the authority so that whatever he bound on earth would be bound in heaven, and whatever he loosed on earth would be loosed in heaven.

The reason why Peter received amazing blessing

What was the reason Peter received such an amazing blessing? While staying near Jesus as His disciple he saw countless works of power manifested through Jesus. Things that could not be done with human ability took place through Jesus. Things that could not be taught by human wisdom were proclaimed through the mouth of Jesus. So, what would those who truly believe in God and have goodness in their heart do? Wouldn't have they recognized Him thinking, 'This is not just an ordinary man but the Son of God who came from heaven'?

But seeing this Jesus, so many people at that time did not recognize Him. Especially, the high priests, priests, the Pharisees, the scribes, and other leaders did not want to acknowledge Him.

But rather some were envious and jealous of Him and tried to kill Him. Still others judged and condemned Him with their own thoughts. Jesus felt so pitiful about those people and said in John 10:25-26, *"I told you, and you do not believe; the works that I do in My Father's name, these testify of Me. But you do not believe because you are not of My sheep."*

Even at the time of Jesus, so many people judged and condemned Jesus and tried to kill Him. However, His disciples, who had been constantly observing Him, were different. Of course, not all the disciples believed and professed Jesus as the Son of God and the Christ deep inside their heart. But, they did believe and acknowledged Jesus.

Peter said to Jesus, *"You are the Christ, the Son of the living God,"* and it was not something he heard from somebody or realized in his thoughts. He could understand it because he saw the works of God that followed Jesus and because God let him realize it.

Practice the Word if you believe Jesus as your Savior

Some say with their lips, "I believe," only because other people tell them that we are saved if we believe in Jesus and we can be healed and receive blessings if we attend church. Of course, when you come to church for the first time, chances are you are not coming to church because you know enough and believe enough. Upon hearing that they could be blessed and saved if they attend church, many people think, 'Why don't I just give it a try?'

But no matter what reason you came to church, after seeing God's wondrous works you should never have the same mind as before. I am saying that you should not just profess with your lips that you believe while not having any faith, but you should accept Jesus Christ as your personal Savior and deliver Jesus Christ to others through your actions.

In my case, I lived a completely different life since I met the living God and accepted Jesus as my personal Savior. I could believe in God and Jesus as my personal Savior 100% in my heart.

I always acknowledged the Lord in my life and obeyed the Word of God. I did not insist on my thoughts, theories, or opinions but just relied on God alone in everything. As said in Proverbs 3:6, *"In all your ways acknowledge Him, and He will make your paths straight,"* because I acknowledged God in everything, God guided me in all my ways.

Then I began to receive amazing blessings like the ones that Peter received. As Jesus said to Peter, *"...whatever you bind on earth shall have been bound in heaven, and whatever you loose on earth shall have been loosed in heaven."* God answered whatever I believed and asked for.

I acknowledged God and got rid of all kinds of evil according to God's Word. When I reached the level of sanctification, God gave me His power. When I laid my hands on the sick, diseases left and they were healed. When I prayed for those who had family or business problems, their problems were solved. As I acknowledged God in everything, confessed my faith, and pleased Him by practicing His Word, He answered all the desires of my heart and blessed me abundantly.

To receive answers before Jesus

In the Bible we see that many people came before Jesus, and their diseases and infirmities were healed or their problems were solved. There were some Gentiles among them, but the majority was the Jews who had believed in God for generations.

But even though they believed in God, they could not solve their problems themselves or receive the answer with their own faith. They were healed of diseases and infirmities and their problems were solved when they came before Jesus. It was because they believed and recognized Jesus and showed the evidence of it with their actions.

The reason why so many people tried to come before Jesus and even touch His clothes is because they had the faith that Jesus was not an ordinary person and their problems would be solved once they went before Him, although their faith was not complete. They could not receive the answers to the problems with their own faith, but they could still receive the answer when they believed, acknowledged and came before Jesus.

How about you, then? If you really believe in Jesus Christ and say, "You are the Christ, the Son of the living God," then God will answer you, seeing your heart. Of course, the confession of faith of those who have been attending church for quite some time should be different from that of new believers. It is because God requires different kinds of confession of the lips from different people according to each individual's faith. Just as knowledge of a four-year-old child and that of a young adult is different, the confession of lips must be different, too.

However, you cannot realize these things by yourself or just hear about it from somebody else and realize. The Holy Spirit in you has to give you the understanding, and you have to confess with the inspiration of the Holy Spirit.

Receiving answers through the confession of lips

In the Bible, there are many people who received their answers by confessing their faith. In Luke chapter 18, when a blind man believed and acknowledged the Lord, came before Him, and confessed, *"Lord, I want to regain my sight"* (v. 41). Jesus replied, *"Receive your sight; your faith has made you well"* (v. 42), and he could see immediately.

When they believed, recognized, came before Jesus and confessed with faith, Jesus sounded forth the original voice and the answer was granted. Jesus has the same power as the omnipotent and omniscient God. If Jesus just decides upon something in His mind, any kind of disease or infirmity will be healed and even all kinds of problems will be solved.

But that doesn't mean He solved anybody's problems and answered just anybody's prayer. It is not right according to justice to pray for and bless those who did not believe, recognize, or take any interest in Him.

Likewise, even if Peter believed and recognized the Lord in his heart, if he did not confess it with his lips, would Jesus still have given Peter those wondrous words of blessing? Jesus could give Peter a promise of blessing without breaking the justice because Peter believed and acknowledged Jesus in his heart and confessed it with his lips.

If you would like to participate in the ministry of the Holy Spirit like Peter did for Jesus, you should make confession of lips that comes out from the depth of your heart. Through such profession of lips stemming from the inspiration of the Holy Spirit, I hope you will receive even the desires of your hearts quickly.

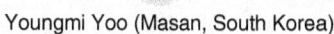

Youngmi Yoo (Masan, South Korea)

Uninvited and unfamiliar disease that came to me one day

In the mid-January of 2005, my left eye suddenly began to dim out and the sight of both eyes weakened. Objects looked vague or almost invisible. Many objects seemed yellow and straight lines appeared curved and waved. Still worse, vomiting and dizziness followed.
The doctor said to me, "It's Harada Disease. Objects look lumpy because there are little lumps in your eyes." He said the cause of the disease was not yet known and the eyesight was not easy to recover with medical treatment. If tumors increased, they would cover the eye's nerves and it would cause me to lose my sight. I began to look back at myself in prayer. Then, I became rather thankful that I would have remained arrogant unless I had that kind of problem.

Afterwards, through the prayer of Rev. Dr. Jaerock Lee on the broadcasts and with the prayer handkerchief which he had prayed

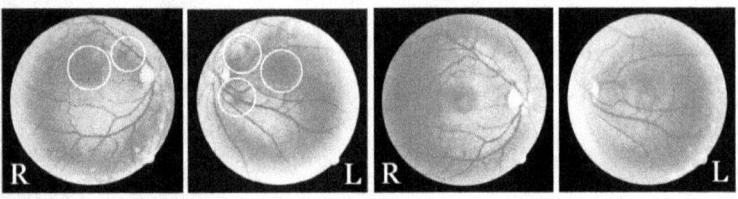

Before prayer   Tumors gone right after prayer

on, my dizziness and vomiting were gone. "**Dead eye nerves, revive! Light, come!**"

Later I found myself watching Friday all-night service on TV with perfect eyesight. Subtitles looked clear to my eyes. I could focus on what I wanted to see, and objects did not appear vague any longer. Colors of each object became clear. Nothing looked yellow at all. Hallelujah!
On February 14, I went for a re-examination to ascertain my healing and glorify God. The doctor said, "Amazing! Your eyes are normal." The doctor knew about the serious conditions of my eyes, and he was surprised that they were normal. After a close examination, he confirmed that the tumors disappeared and swelling was gone.

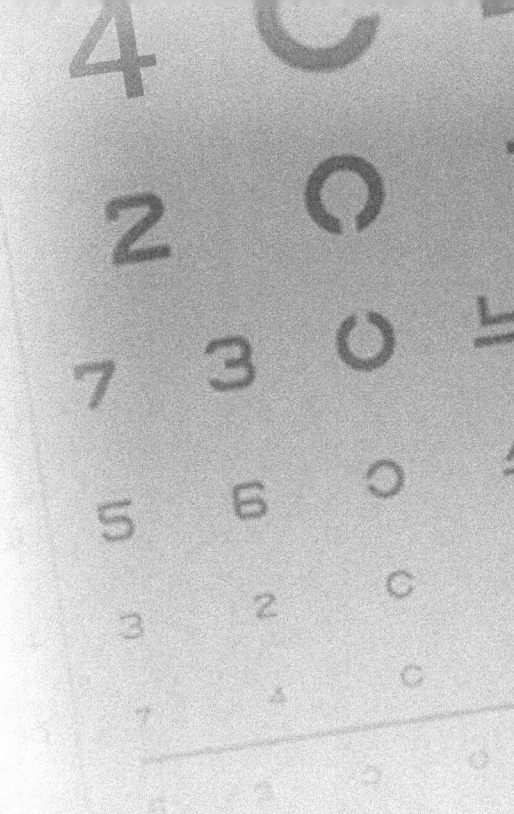

He asked me whether I had received medical treatment at another hospital. I gave him a clear answer: "No. I just received the prayer of Rev. Dr. Lee and was healed by the power of God."

My eyesight used to be 0.8/0.25 before I received the prayer, but it was improved to show 1.0/1.0 after the prayer. Now my sight is 1.2 in both eyes.

- Extract from Extraordinary Things -

Chapter 8: What do you want Me to do for you?

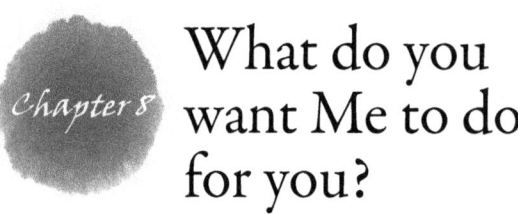

> "When Jesus said,
> *"What do you want Me to do for you?"*
> it was that He sounded forth the original voice.

To receive the answer through the original voice

Trust Jesus from the depth of the heart

Cry out when asking God

Perfect faith that does not waver

Throw away your cloak

God hears the confession of faith

"What do you want Me to do for you?"
And he said, "Lord, I want to regain my sight!"
———————

Luke 18:41

Even those who come to church for the first time can still receive the answer to any kind of problem if they just trust God in their inner heart. It is because God is our good Father who wants to give good things to His children, as written in Matthew 7:11, *"If you then, being evil, know how to give good gifts to your children, how much more will your Father who is in heaven give what is good to those who ask Him!"*

The reason why God has made the conditions to receive the answer in His justice is to let His beloved children receive abundant blessings. God did not set the conditions to say, "I cannot give to you because you fail to meet the standards."

He teaches us the ways to receive the answer to desires of our heart, financial problems, family problems, or problems of diseases. And, to receive such answers in God's justice, faith and obedience are the most important.

To receive the answer through the original voice

In Luke chapter 18, we read about the details of a blind man who received his answer when Jesus sounded forth the original voice. He heard Jesus was passing by while he was begging on the streets, and he called out with a loud voice. *"Jesus, Son of David, have mercy on me!"* Those who led the way were sternly telling him to be quiet; but he kept crying out all the more, *"Son of David, have mercy on me!"*

And Jesus stopped and commanded that he be brought to Him; and He questioned him, *"What do you want Me to do for you?"* And he said, *"Lord, I want to regain my sight!"* And Jesus said to him, *"Receive your sight; your faith has made you well."* As soon as Jesus said it, an extraordinary work took place. Immediately he regained his sight. And when all the people saw it, they gave praise to God.

When Jesus said, *"What do you want Me to do for you?"* He was sounding forth the original voice. When the blind man said, *"Lord, I want to regain my sight!"* and the Lord said, *"...your faith has made you well"*, it was original voice once again.

'Original Voice' is the voice of God that He spoke forth when He created heavens and earth and all things in them with His Word. This blind man could receive sight when Jesus sounded forth the original voice because he met the proper conditions to receive the answer. From this point on, let us examine in detail how this blind man could receive his answer.

Trust Jesus deep in the heart

Jesus went into towns and cities, spread the gospel of the kingdom of heaven and confirmed His Word with signs and wonders that followed. The disabled came to walk, lepers were healed and those who had visual or audio impairment came to see and hear. Those who couldn't speak came to speak, and the demons were driven out. Because the news about Jesus was widespread, a crowd of people gathered around Jesus wherever He went.

One day, Jesus went to Jericho. As usual, a lot of people gathered around Jesus and followed Him. At this time, a blind man who was sitting on the street begging heard a crowd passing by and asked people what was happening. Somebody told him, *"Jesus of Nazareth is passing by."* Then, this blind man, without hesitation, shouted, *"Jesus, Son of David, have mercy on me!"*

The reason why he could call out in this way was because he believed that Jesus could certainly make him see. Also, it is inferred that he believed Jesus as the Savior from the fact that he called out, *"Jesus, Son of David."*

It is because all the people in Israel knew that the Messiah would come in the family of David. The first reason this blind man could receive the answer is because he believed and accepted Jesus as the Savior. He also believed without question that this Jesus could make him see.

Although he was blind and could not see, he heard a lot of news about Jesus. He heard that a person called Jesus had appeared, and He had such mighty power that He solved any kind of problem that no other man could solve.

As said in Romans 10:17, *"So faith comes from hearing,"* this blind man came to have faith that he would receive the sight if he could just go to Jesus. He could believe what he heard because he had relatively good heart.

Likewise, if we have good heart, it is easier for us to have spiritual faith when we hear the gospel. Gospel is 'good news', and the news about Jesus was also good news. So those with good hearts just accept the good news. For example, when somebody says, "I am healed of an incurable disease through prayer," those with good hearts will rejoice with him. Even if they do not believe it completely, they would think, "It is a really good thing if it's true."

The more evil people are, the more they doubt and try not to believe it. Some even judge or condemn saying, "They are making it up to deceive people." But if they say the works of the Holy Spirit manifested by God are falsehood and fabrication, this is blaspheming the Holy Spirit.

Matthew 12:31-32 says, *"Therefore I say to you, any sin and blasphemy shall be forgiven people, but blasphemy against the Spirit shall not be forgiven. Whoever speaks a word against the Son of Man, it shall be forgiven him; but whoever speaks against the Holy Spirit, it shall not be forgiven him, either in this age or in the age to come."*

If you condemned a church that shows works of the Holy Spirit you have to repent. Only when the wall of sin between God and you is removed, and will you be able to receive the answer.

1 John 1:9 says, *"If we confess our sins, He is faithful and righteous to forgive us our sins and to cleanse us from all unrighteousness."* If you have anything to repent of, I hope you will repent thoroughly before God with tears and walk only in the Light.

Cry out when asking God

When the blind man heard Jesus was passing by, he called out, saying, *"Jesus, Son of David, have mercy on me!"* He cried out to Jesus in a loud voice. Why did he have to cry out in a loud voice?

Genesis 3:17 says, *"Then to Adam He said, 'Because you have listened to the voice of your wife, and have eaten from the tree about which I commanded you, saying, 'You shall not eat from it'; cursed is the ground because of you; in toil you will eat of it all the days of your life.'"*

Before the first man Adam ate from the tree of the knowledge of good and evil, people could eat what God provided as much as they wanted. However, after Adam disobeyed God's Word and ate from the tree, sin came into men and we became men of flesh. From that time on, we could eat only through painful toil.

This is the justice set by God. Therefore, only by the sweat of our brows we can receive answers from God. Namely, we have to toil in our prayer with all our heart, mind, and soul and cry out to receive the answer.

Jeremiah 33:3 says, *"Call to Me and I will answer you, and I will tell you great and mighty things, which you do not know."* Luke 22:44 says, *"And being in agony He was praying very fervently; and His sweat became like drops of blood, falling down upon the ground."*

Also, in John 11, when Jesus revived Lazarus who had been dead for four days, He called out in a loud voice, *"Lazarus, come forth!"* (John 11:43). When Jesus shed all His water and blood and breathed His last on the cross, He, crying out with a loud voice, said, *"Father, into Your hands I commit My spirit"* (Luke 23:46).

Because He came to this earth in human flesh, even sinless Jesus cried out with a loud voice, so that it was in accordance with God's justice. How could, then, we creatures of God, just sit down and pray in an easy way without crying out loudly to receive the answer to problems that cannot be solved by human ability? Therefore, the second reason why the blind man could receive the answer was because he cried out in a loud voice, which was the way in accordance with God's justice.

Jacob received blessing of God as he prayed until the socket of his thigh was dislocated (Genesis 32:24-30). Until there was rain to end the three-and-a-half-year drought, Elijah prayed so earnestly his head was put between his knees, (1 Kings 18:42-46). We can receive the answer quickly by moving God's heart when we pray with all our strength, faith, and love.

To cry out in prayer does not mean we have to scream with an annoying voice. You can refer to the proper ways of prayer and the way to receive God's answers in the book, 'Keep Watching and Praying'.

Perfect faith that does not waver

Some people say, "God knows even the deepest part of your heart, so you do not have to cry out in your prayer." But that is not true. The blind man was sternly told to be quiet, but he kept crying out all the more.

He did not obey the people who were telling him to be quiet, but he shouted all the more according to the justice of God with an even more passionate heart. His faith at this moment was perfect faith that would not be changed. And the third reason why he received the answer is because he showed his faith that was unchanging in any kind of situation.

When the people rebuked him, if the blind man had been offended or had kept quiet, he would not have received his sight. However, because he had such firm faith that he would be able to see once he met Jesus, he could not miss that moment despite people's rebukes. It was not a time to show his pride. Or he could not yield to any kind of hardship. He kept on crying earnestly and finally received the answer.

In Matthew chapter 15 is an account of a Canaanite woman who came with a humble heart before Jesus and received the answer. When Jesus went to Tyre and Sidon, a woman came before Him asking Him to drive away a demon that possessed her daughter. What did Jesus say then? He said, *"It is not good to take the children's bread and throw it to the dogs."* The children referred to the people of Israel and the Canaanite woman, a dog.

Ordinary people would have been very offended by such a remark and would have gone away. But she was different. She humbly asked for mercy saying, *"Yes, Lord; but even the dogs feed on the crumbs which fall from their masters' table."* Jesus was moved and said, *"O woman, your faith is great; it shall be done for you as you wish."* Immediately her daughter was healed. She received the answer because she threw away all her pride and humbled herself completely.

However, many people, even though they come before God to solve a big problem, just go back or do not rely upon God, only because their feelings were hurt by some small thing. But if they really have the faith to solve any difficult problem, then with a humble heart, they would just keep on asking God for His grace.

Throw away your cloak

When Jesus went into Jericho at that time, He opened the eyes of a blind man, and from Mark 10:46-52, we read that

Jesus opened the eyes of another blind man. This blind man was Bartimaeus.

He also called out in a loud voice upon hearing that Jesus was passing by. Jesus told the people to bring him, and we have to pay attention to what he did. Mark 10:50 says, *"Throwing aside his cloak, he jumped up and came to Jesus."* This is the reason that he could receive the answer: he threw away his cloak and came to Jesus.

What, then, is the spiritual meaning hidden in throwing away his cloak that it was one of the conditions to receive the answer? The cloak of the beggar must have been dirty and stinky. But it is the only possession of the beggar with which he could protect his body. But Bartimaeus had a good heart that he could not go before Jesus with his dirty and stinky cloak.

Jesus, whom he was going to meet, was such a holy and clean person. The blind man knew that Jesus was such a good man who gave grace to people, healed them, and gave hope to the poor and the sick. So he listened to the voice of his conscience that he could not go before Jesus with his dirty and stinky cloak. He obeyed the voice and threw it away.

It was before Bartimaeus received the Holy Spirit, so he listened to the voice of his good conscience and obeyed it. Namely, he threw away his most precious possession, his cloak, immediately. Another spiritual meaning of the cloak is our heart that is dirty and smells foul. It is the heart of untruth such as pride, arrogance, and all other dirty things.

This implies that, in order to meet God who is holy, we have to throw away all dirty and stinky sins, which are like the dirty cloak of the beggar. If you truly want to receive the answer, you must listen to the voice of the Holy Spirit when the Holy Spirit reminds you of your past sins. And, you have to repent each of them. You should obey without hesitation what the voice of the Holy Spirit tells you- the way the blind man Bartimaeus did.

God hears the confession of faith

Jesus finally answered to this blind man who was asking with full assurance of faith. Jesus asked him, *"What do you want Me to do for you?"* Didn't Jesus know what this blind man wanted? Of course, He did, but the reason why He still asked is because there must be a confession of faith. It is God's justice that we have to make the confession of our faith with our lips in order to receive the actual answer.

Jesus asked the blind man *"What do you want Me to do for you?"* because he had met the conditions to be able to receive the answer. As he answered, *"Lord, I want to regain my sight!"* it was granted him. Likewise, if only we meet the conditions according to the justice of God, we can receive anything that we ask.

Do you know the story about the magic lamp of Aladdin? Supposedly, if you rubbed the lamp three times, a giant would come out of the lamp and make three wishes of yours come true. Though this is just a story made by people, we have a much more wondrous and powerful key for answers. In John 15:7 Jesus said, *"If you abide in Me, and My words abide in you, ask whatever you wish, and it will be done for you."*

Do you believe in the power of the almighty God the Father who is omnipotent? Then, you can just abide in the Lord and let the Word abide in you. I hope you will be one with the Lord through faith and obedience, so that you will be able to boldly profess your desires and receive them as the original voice is sounded forth.

Ms. Akiyo Hirouchi (Maizuru, Japan)

My Grand-daughter's atrial septal defect was healed!

In the beginning of 2005, twin sisters were born in our family. But after about 3 months, the second of the twins had difficulty breathing. She was diagnosed with an atrial septal defect with a 4.5-mm puncture in her heart. She could not hold her head still nor could she suck milk. The milk had to be supplied through her nose by a tube.

It was critical and a pediatrician of Kyoto University hospital came all the way to Maizuru citizen's hospital. The baby's body was too weak to be transferred to the university hospital which was a good distance away. So she just had to receive treatment there in the local hospital.
Pastor Keontae Kim of Osaka & Maizuru Manmin church prayed for her with a handkerchief on which Rev. Jaerock Lee had prayed.

Also, he sent a prayer request to the main church in Seoul along with her photo.

I was not in a situation to be able to attend the worship service on the Internet, so we recorded the Friday all-night service of Manmin Central Church on June 10, 2005, and then the whole family together received the prayer of Rev. Lee.

"Father God, heal her transcending space and time. Lay Your hands on Miki Yuna, grand-daughter of Hirouchi Akiyo in Japan. Atrial septal defect, go away! Be burned by the fire of the Holy Spirit and be healthy!"

The next day, June 11, a wondrous thing took place. The baby had not been able to breathe on her own, but she got better and they could take away the respirator.

"It is a miracle that the baby recovered this fast!" The doctor was amazed.

Since then, the baby grew up very well. She had weighed only 2.4 kg but within 2 months from the time she received the prayer, the weight was 5 kg! Her voice when crying was much stronger, too. Seeing this miracle firsthand, I registered in Manmin Central Church in August 2005. I realized that He granted a divine healing work knowing that I would believe in Him through the miracle.

Through this grace, I devotedly worked to establish a Manmin church in Maizuru. Three years after the opening, the church members and I offered to God to buy a beautiful sanctuary building. Today, I am doing many voluntary works for the kingdom of God. I am thankful, not just for the healing grace of my grand-daughter, but also for the grace of God leading me to the way of true life.

- Extract from *Extraordinary Things* -

Chapter 1: "It shall be done for you as you have believed"

> The original voice that comes out
> from the mouth of Jesus
> goes throughout the earth
> and reaches the end of the world,
> thereby manifesting His power
> transcending time and space.

All creatures obey the original voice

Men became unable to hear the original voice

Reason why they do not get answers

The centurion had a good heart

The centurion experienced a miracle transcending time and space

Powerful works transcending time and space

*"And Jesus said to the centurion,
'Go; it shall be done for you as you have believed.'
And the servant was healed that very moment."*

Matthew 8:13

When they are in agony or in difficulties where there seems to be no way out, many people feel that God is far away from them or is turning His face away from them. Some of them even doubt thinking, 'Does God even know that I am here?' or 'Does God listen to my prayers when I pray?' This is because they do not have enough faith in the omnipotent and omniscient God.

David had gone through so many hardships in life and yet he professed, *"If I ascend to heaven, You are there; if I make my bed in Sheol, behold, You are there. I take the wings of the dawn, if I dwell in the remotest part of the sea, even there Your hand will lead me, and Your right hand will lay hold of me"* (Psalm 139:8-10).

Because God rules over the whole universe and all things in them beyond time and space, the physical distance that human beings feel is of no consequence to God at all.

Isaiah 57:19 says, *""I create the fruit of the lips: Peace, peace to him who is far off and to him who is near,' says the LORD, 'And I will heal him'"* (NKJV). Here, 'I create the fruit of the lips' means the word given forth by God will certainly be fulfilled, as said in Numbers 23:19.

Isaiah 55:11 also says, *"So will My word be which goes forth from My mouth; it will not return to Me empty, without accomplishing what I desire, and without succeeding in the matter for which I sent it."*

All creatures obey the original voice

God the Creator created the heavens and the earth with

His original voice. Thus, all that was created by the original voice obey the original voice even though they are not living organisms. For example, today we have voice-recognition devices that respond to only a certain voice. In the same way, the original voice is embedded in all things in the universe, so that they obey when the original voice is sounded forth.

Jesus, who is in very nature God, sounded forth the original voice as well. Mark 4:39 says, *"And He got up and rebuked the wind and said to the sea, 'Hush, be still.' And the wind died down and it became perfectly calm."* Even the sea and wind that have no ear or life obey the original voice. What, then, should we human beings who have ears and rationality, do? We obviously have to obey. But then, what is the reason that people do not obey?

In the example of a voice-recognition device, let us suppose there are one hundred machines of this kind. The owner set the machines to operate when they hear the voice say, "Yes." But somebody changed the setting on 40 machines. He set 40 of the machines to operate when they hear "No." Then, these 40 machines will never operate even when the owner says "Yes." In much the same way, since Adam sinned, men became unable to hear the original voice.

Men became unable to hear the original voice

Adam was actually created as a living spirit, and listened to and obeyed only God's Word, the truth. God the Father taught Adam only spiritual knowledge, which was the words of truth, but since God gave Adam freewill it was up to Adam to decide whether he would obey the truth or not. God did not want a child who is like a robot who would unconditionally obey all the time.

He wanted children who would voluntarily obey His Word and love Him with true hearts. However, after a long time passed, Adam was tempted by Satan and he disobeyed God's Word.

Romans 6:16 says, *"Do you not know that when you present yourselves to someone as slaves for obedience, you are slaves of the one whom you obey, either of sin resulting in death, or of obedience resulting in righteousness?"* As said, Adam's descendants became the slaves of sin and of the enemy devil and Satan, due to his disobedience.

They were now destined to think, speak, and act as Satan instigated them, and they were to add sins upon sins and finally fall into death. However, Jesus came to this earth in the providence of God. He died as the propitiation to redeem all sinners, and He resurrected.

For this reason, Romans 8:2 says, *"For the law of the Spirit of life in Christ Jesus has set you free from the law of sin and of death."* As said, those who believe in Jesus Christ in their heart and walk in the Light are no more slaves of sin.

It means they have been enabled to hear the original voice of God through their faith in Jesus Christ. Therefore, those who hear it and obey it can receive the answer to whatever they ask.

Reason why they do not get answers

Now, some people might ask, "I believe in Jesus Christ and have been forgiven of sins, and why am I not getting healed?" Then, I would like to ask you this question: To what extent have you obeyed God's Word in the Bible?

While you profess you believe in God, haven't you loved

the world, cheated others, or done bad things just like secular people? I'd like you to check if you have kept all the Sundays holy, given proper tithes, and obeyed all God's commands that tell us to do, not do, keep, or cast away certain things.

If you can confidently say yes to the above questions, you will receive the answer to whatever you ask. Even if the answer is delayed, you will just give thanks from the depths of your heart and rely on God without wavering. If you show your faith this way, God will not hesitate to grant the answer. He will sound forth the original voice and say, "It shall be done for you as you have believed," and it will actually be done according to your faith.

The centurion had a good heart

In Matthew chapter 8, there is an account of a Roman centurion who received an answer through faith. When he came to Jesus, his servant's disease was healed through the original voice sounded forth by Jesus.

At that time, Israel was under the rule of the Roman Empire. There were commanders over thousands, hundreds, fifties and tens in the Roman army. Their title of rank was according to the number of soldiers they commanded. One of those who were in charge of a hundred soldiers, a Centurion, was in Capernaum of Israel. He heard news about Jesus that He taught love, goodness, and mercy.

Jesus taught in Matthew 5:38-39 *"You have heard that it was said, 'An eye for an eye, and a tooth for a tooth.' But I say to you, do not resist an evil person; but whoever slaps you on your right cheek, turn the other to him also."*

Also, He said in Matthew 5:43-44, *"You have heard that it*

was said, 'You shall love your neighbor and hate your enemy.' But I say to you, love your enemies and pray for those who persecute you." Those who are good in heart will be moved when they hear such words of goodness as this.

But the centurion also heard that Jesus did not only teach goodness but also performed signs and wonders that could not be done with human abilities. The news was that lepers, who were considered to be cursed, were healed, the blind came to see, the mute came to speak, and the deaf came to hear. Furthermore, the lame came to walk and leap and the crippled also walked. And the centurion just believed those words as they were.

But different people responded differently towards such news about Jesus. When they saw God's works, the first type of people did not have understanding. Because of their firmly self-centered frameworks of faith, instead of accepting and believing, they passed judgment and condemnation.

The Pharisees and the scribes, who had the vested rights, were this type. In Matthew 12:24 it is recorded that they even spoke of Jesus saying, *"This man casts out demons only by Beelzebul the ruler of the demons."* They spoke evil words with their spiritual ignorance.

The second type of people believed Jesus as one of the great prophets and followed Him. For example, when Jesus raised a young man from the dead, people said, *"Fear gripped them all, and they began glorifying God, saying, 'A great prophet has arisen among us!' and, 'God has visited His people!'"* (Luke 7:16)

Now, thirdly, there were people who realized in their heart and believed that Jesus is the Son of God who came to this earth to become the Savior for all men. A man was blind from birth, but his eyes were opened when he met Jesus. He said, *"Since the beginning of time it has never been heard that anyone opened the eyes of a person born blind. If this man were not from God, He could do nothing"* (John 9:32-33).

He realized that Jesus came as the Savior. He confessed, "Lord, I believe," and he worshiped Jesus. Likewise, those who had a good heart that was able to recognize something good could realize that Jesus is the Son of God just by seeing what Jesus did.

In John 14:11 Jesus said, *"Believe Me that I am in the Father and the Father is in Me; otherwise believe because of the works themselves."* If you had lived at the time of Jesus, what kind of people do you think you would have belonged to?

The centurion was one of the people among the third type. He believed the news about Jesus as it was and he went before Him.

The centurion experienced a miracle transcending time and space

What is the reason that the centurion received the answer he wanted, immediately after he heard Jesus say, "It shall be done for you as you have believed"?

We can see that the centurion trusted Jesus in his heart. He could obey whatever Jesus would tell him. But the most important thing about this centurion is that he came before Jesus with true love for souls.

Matthew 8:6 says, *"Lord, my servant is lying paralyzed at home, fearfully tormented."* This centurion came before Jesus and asked not for his own parents, relatives, or even his own children, but for his servant. He took the pain of his servant as his own pain and came before Jesus, and how would Jesus not be moved by his good heart?

Paralysis is a severe condition which cannot easily be cured even with finest of medical skills. One cannot move his hands and feet freely, so he needs to get others' help. Also, in some cases one has to get help from others to wash, eat, or change his clothes.

If the disease persists for a long time, it is very hard to find a person who can unchangingly take care of the sick person with love and compassion, as the old Korean saying goes, "There are no devoted sons in long disease." There are not many who can love their own family members as themselves.

However, sometimes when the whole family earnestly prays for them with love, we can see those who went beyond the limit of life getting healed or receiving the answer to a very difficult problem. Their prayer and deeds of love move the heart of God the Father so much that God shows them love that goes beyond His justice.

The centurion had such complete trust in Jesus that He could heal his servant's paralysis. He asked Jesus and received the answer.

The second reason that the centurion could receive the answer was because he showed perfect faith and willingness to obey Jesus completely.

Jesus saw that the centurion loved his servant as himself and said to him, *"I will come and heal him."* But the centurion said in Matthew 8:8, *"Lord, I am not worthy for You to come under my roof, but just say the word, and my servant will be healed."*

For most people, they would be very happy that Jesus would come to their home. But for the centurion, he boldly professed as above because he had true faith.

It was because he had the kind of attitude to obey whatever

Jesus would have said. We can see that from his word in Matthew 8:9 that says *"For I also am a man under authority, with soldiers under me; and I say to this one, 'Go!' and he goes, and to another, 'Come!' and he comes, and to my slave, 'Do this!' and he does it."* Now when Jesus heard this, He marveled and said to those who were following, *"Truly I say to you, I have not found such great faith with anyone in Israel."*

In the same way, if you did what God tells us to do, did not do what God tells us not to do, kept what God tells us to keep, and threw away what God tells us to throw away, you can be confident and ask for anything before God. It's because 1 John 3:21-22 says, *"Beloved, if our heart does not condemn us, we have confidence before God; and whatever we ask we receive from Him, because we keep His commandments and do the things that are pleasing in His sight."*

The centurion had perfect faith in the power of Jesus who could heal by just using His Word. Even though he was a centurion of the Roman Empire, he humbled himself and had the willingness to obey Jesus completely. For these reasons, he received the answer to his desire.

In Matthew 8:13, Jesus said to the centurion, *"Go; it shall be done for you as you have believed,"* and the servant was healed that very moment. When Jesus sounded forth the original voice, the answer was given transcending space and time, just as the centurion had believed.

Powerful works transcending time and space

Psalm 19:4 says, *"...yet their voice goes out through all the earth, and their words to the end of the world..."* (NRSV) As said, the original voice that came out of Jesus' mouth could reach the ends of the world, and God's power was manifested beyond space regardless of the physical distance.

Also, once the original voice is sounded forth, it transcends time. Therefore, even after some time, the word is accomplished once our vessel to receive the answer is ready.

So many works of God's power beyond time and space are taking place in this church. In 1999, there was a sister of a Pakistani girl who came to me with the photo of her sister named Cynthia. At that time, Cynthia was dying from narrowing of the large intestine as well as Celiac disease.

The doctor said there was little chance of survival even with the operation. In this situation, Cynthia's elder sister came to me with her sister's photo to receive my prayer. From the moment I prayed for Cynthia, she recovered very quickly.

In October 2003, an assistant pastor's wife of our church came to receive my prayer on her brother's photo. Her brother had a problem with the number of his blood platelets decreasing. He had blood in his urine, stool, eyes, nose, and mouth. His blood also went into his lungs and intestines. He was just waiting for death. But when I prayed with my hands on his photo, the number of platelets quickly went up, and he recovered very quickly.

These kinds of works beyond time and space took place so much in the Russian crusade held in St. Petersburg in November 2003. The crusade was broadcast through 12 satellites to more than 150 countries throughout Russia, Europe, Asia, North America, and Latin America. Broadcasting included India, the Philippines, Australia, the United States, Honduras and Peru. Also, simultaneous screen meetings were held in 4 other cities of

Russia and in Kiev, Ukraine.

Whether people attended the screen meetings or watched it on TV at home, those who listened to the message and received the prayer with faith received healing at the same time and sent us testimonies through emails and so on. Although they were not in the same physical space when the original voice was sounded forth, the voice worked on them as well because they were together in the same spiritual space.

If you just have true faith and willingness to obey God's Word, show your true acts of love like the centurion, and believe in the power of God who works transcending time and space, you can live a blessed life, receiving answers to whatever you ask.

In the Two-week Continuous Special Revival Meetings, which were held for 12 years from 1993 to 2004, people were healed of various kinds of diseases and received solutions to various life problems. Others were led to the way of salvation. However, God made us stop these revival meetings after the 2004 revival meeting. It was for an even greater leap forward.

God let me begin new spiritual studies and began explaining to me a different dimension of the spiritual realm. I could not understand what was meant initially. There were completely new terms, too. But I just obeyed and began to learn them believing I would someday understand.

About 30 years ago, I received the power of God through so much prayer and fasting that I had offered since I became a pastor. I had to struggle against extremely hot and cold during 10, 21, 40 days of fasting and praying to God.

But the spiritual studies that God gave me were incomparably more painful training than those efforts. I had to try to understand the things that I had never heard before, and I had to pray like Jacob at Jabbok River until I did understand them.

Furthermore, I also had to suffer from various physical conditions of my body. Just like an astronaut would have to be trained very well to adapt to the life in the space, there were different things taking place in my body until I reached a dimension that God wanted me to reach.

But I overcame each moment with my love and faith in God, and soon enough I acquired spiritual knowledge about the origin of the Father God, and the law of love and justice, and many others.

In addition, the closer I got to the dimension that God wanted me to reach, the powerful works took place increasingly more greatly. The speed of the church members receiving blessings became much faster, as well as the speed of divine healings taking place. There are increasingly more testimonies day by day.

God wants to fulfill His providence at the end time with the highest and greatest power that men cannot imagine. For this reason He gave this power, so the Grand Sanctuary would be built as the ark of salvation that will proclaim the glory of God, and the gospel would be carried back to Israel.

It is extremely difficult to preach the gospel in Israel. They do not allow any Christian gathering there. It can be done only by tremendous power of God that can even shake the world, and it is the duty given to our church to preach the gospel in Israel.

I just hope that you will realize the time is very near for God to wrap up all His end time plans, try to adorn yourself as brides of the Lord, and make everything go well with you, even as your soul prospers.

Third heaven and space of the third dimension

The fourth heaven is the space exclusively for the original God.
It is a place for God the Trinity and everything is possible there.
Things are created from nothing.
As God harbors something in His heart it is done.
Even the solid objects can turn freely into liquid or gas.
The space that has such characters is called 'the space of the fourth dimension'.

The works utilizing this spiritual space of the fourth dimension include works of creation, controlling life and death, healing and other works transcending time and space. The power of God who possesses the fourth heaven is being manifested today as it was yesterday.

1. Works of Creation

A work of creation is to create something for the first time that never existed before. It was the work of creation when God created the heavens and earth and all things in them in the beginning with only His Word. God can show the works of creation because He possesses the fourth heaven.

Works of creation manifested by Jesus

Changing water into wine, in John chapter 2, is a work of creation. Jesus was invited to a wedding banquet, and the wine ran out.
Mary felt sorry for this situation and asked Jesus for help. Jesus declined at first, but Mary still had faith. She believed that Jesus would help the host of the banquet.
Jesus considered the perfect faith of Mary and told the servants to fill the water pots with water and take them to the headwaiter. He did not pray or command for the water to be changed into wine. He just harbored it in His heart, and the water in the six water pots turned into high quality wine in a moment.

Works of creation through Elijah

The widow of Zarephath in 1 Kings chapter 17 was in a very difficult situation. Due to a long lasting drought her food ran out and all she had left was a handful of flour and a little oil.
But Elijah asked her to bake a piece of bread and give it to him, saying, *"For thus says the LORD God of Israel, 'The bowl of flour shall not be exhausted, nor shall the jar of oil be empty, until the day that the LORD sends rain on the face of the earth'"* (1 Kings 17:14). The widow obeyed Elijah without giving any excuses.

As a result, she and Elijah and her household ate for many days, but the bowl of flour was not exhausted nor did the jar of oil become empty (1 Kings 17:15-16). Here, the handful of flour and the oil in the jar not running out indicates that works of creation took place.

Works of creation through Moses

In Exodus 15:22-23, we find that the sons of Israel had crossed the Red Sea and came into the wilderness. Three days passed, but they were unable to find any water. They found water at a place called Marah, but it was bitter and not potable. They began to complain loudly.
Now, Moses prayed to God, and God showed him a tree. As Moses threw it into the waters, the waters became sweet and potable. It is not because the tree had some elements that could take the bitter taste away from the water. It was God showing the work of creation that was manifested through Moses' faith and obedience.

Muan Sweet Water Site

Muan Manmin Church experiences works of creation

God is still showing us the works of creation today. Muan sweet water is one such work. On March 4, 2000, I prayed in Seoul that the salty water at Muan Manmin Church would turn into sweet water, and the members of the church confirmed the prayer was answered the next day, on March 5.
Muan Manmin church is surrounded by the sea, and they got only sea water from the well. They had to get drinking water through a pipe from a place 3 km away. It was very inconvenient for them.
The members of Muan Manmin Church remembered the event at Marah in the book of Exodus, and they asked me to pray with faith that the salty water would turn sweet. During my 10-day mountain prayer from February 21, I prayed for Muan Manmin Church. The members of Muan Manmin Church also fasted and prayed for the same.

During my mountain prayer I only focused on the prayers and the Word of God. My effort and the faith of the members of Muan Manmin Church met the conditions of justice of God, and such an amazing work of creation was manifested.

With the spiritual eyes, one is able to see the beam of light from the throne of God that comes all the way down to the end of the pipe of the well, so when the salty water passes that beam it turns into sweet water.

But this Muan sweet water is not just potable. When people drink or apply it with faith, they receive divine healing and answers to problems according to their faith. There are countless testimonies of such works through Muan sweet water, and many people from around the world visit this well at Muan Manmin Church.

Muan sweet water was tested by the Food and Drug Administration of the United States and its safeness and good qualities were confirmed in the five categories of: mineral factors, heavy metal content, chemical residues, skin reaction, and toxicity through experimental mouse. It was especially rich in minerals and its calcium content was more than three times higher than other famous mineral water from France and Germany.

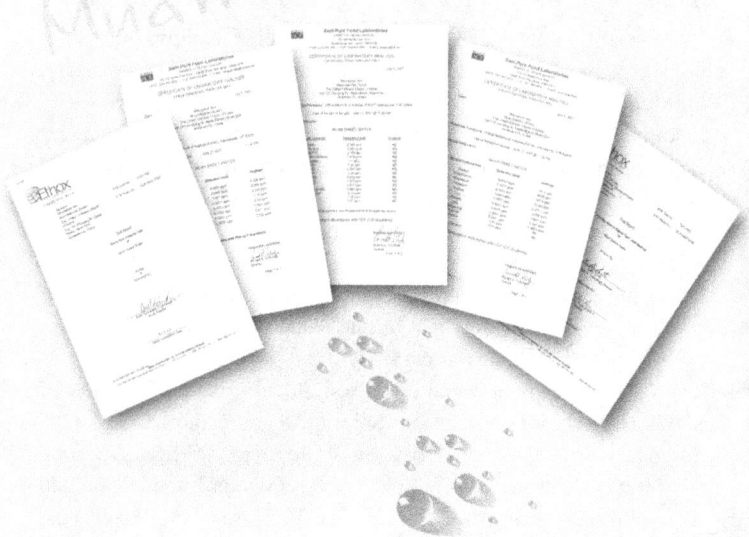

FDA (Food and Drug Administration) test results

2. Controlling Life

In the space of the fourth dimension, which has the characters of the fourth heaven, something dead can be given life, or something alive can be put to death, too. It applies to everything that has life, whether plants or animals.

It was the case with the Aaron's staff that sprouted. It was covered by the space of the fourth dimension. So, within a day's time a dry staff sprouted and put forth buds, produced blossoms, and it bore ripe almonds. In Matthew 21:19, Jesus said to a fig tree that had no fruits, *"no longer shall there ever be any fruit from you."* And at once the fig tree withered. This was also done as the space of the fourth dimension covered it.

In John 11, we read the account of Jesus reviving Lazarus who had been dead for four days and smelled foul. In Lazarus's case, not just his soul had to return, but also his body that had already decayed had to be renewed completely. It was physically impossible, but his body could recover in a moment in the space of the fourth dimension.

In Manmin Central Church, a brother called Keonwi Park had lost the sight in one of his eyes completely, but came to see again. He underwent cataract surgery when he was three. Complications followed and he suffered from serious uveitis and retinal detachment. If the retina is detached, you can't see properly. Furthermore, he also suffered phthisis bulbi, which is the shrinking of the eyeballs. Eventually in 2006 he lost his sight completely in his left eye.

But in July 2007, he received his sight through my prayer. His left eye could not even sense any light but he could now see. The shrunken eyeball also regained its normal size.
The vision in his right eye also was bad, 0.1 in scale, but it improved to 0.9. His testimony was introduced with all the medical and hospital documents in the 5th International Christian Medical Doctors' Conference held in Norway. The conference was attended by 220 medical professionals from 41 countries. The case was selected as the most interesting case among the many other cases presented.

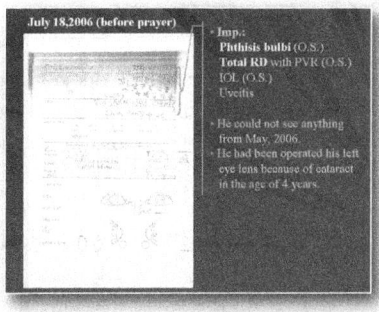

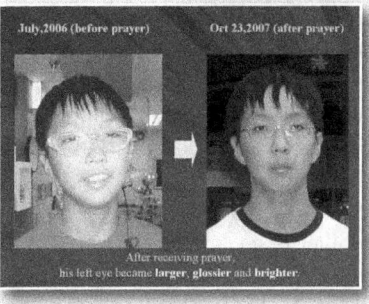

The case of Gunwui Park presented in the 5th WCDN Conference

The same thing can happen for other tissues or nerves. Even though the nerves or the cells are dead, they can be made normal again if the space of the fourth dimension covers them. Physical disabilities can also be made whole in the space of the fourth dimension. Other diseases caused by germs or viruses such as AIDS, tuberculosis, cold, or fever can be healed in the space of the fourth dimension.

In such cases, the fire of the Holy Spirit comes down and burns the germs or the viruses. And the damaged tissues will recover in the space of the fourth heaven, and it is complete healing. Even for the problem of infertility, if the organ or the part that has the problem is fixed in the space of the fourth dimension, one can have a baby. For us to be healed of sicknesses or infirmities by the power of God in the space of the fourth dimension, we have to meet the conditions of the justice of God.

3. Works that Transcend Time and Space

The powerful works taking place in the space of the fourth dimension are manifested transcending time and space. It's because the space of the fourth dimension contain and transcend all the spaces of other dimensions. Psalm 19:4 says, *"...yet their voice goes out through all the earth, and their words to the end of the world..."* (NRSV) It means the words of God dwelling in the fourth heaven will reach the end of the world.

Even two points at a great distance in this first heaven, the physical realm, are like being right next to each other in the concept of the space of the fourth dimension. Light travels around the Earth seven and a half times in a second. But the light of the power of God can reach even the end of the universe in a moment. Therefore, the distance in physical realm has no meaning or limitations in the space of the fourth dimension.

In Matthew chapter 8, a centurion asked Jesus to heal his servant. Jesus said He would go to his house, and the centurion said, *"Lord, I am not worthy for You to come under my roof, but just say the word, and my servant will be healed."* So, Jesus said, *"Go; it shall be done for you as you have believed."* And the servant was healed at that very moment.

Because Jesus possesses the space of the fourth heaven, a sick person who was at a distant place was healed just by the command of Jesus. The centurion received such a blessing because he showed perfect faith in Jesus. Jesus also praised the faith of the centurion saying, *"Truly I say to you, I have not found such great faith with anyone in Israel."*

Even today, for those children who are united with God through perfect faith, God shows the works of power that transcend time and space.

Cynthia in Pakistan was dying of Celiac disease. Lysanias in Israel was dying of viral infection. But they were healed through the power of prayer that transcends time and space. Robert Johnson in the United States also received healing through the power of prayer transcending time and space. His Achilles tendon was ruptured and he could not walk due to severe pain. Without any medical treatment it recovered completely with only the power of prayer transcending time and space. This is the work of power being manifested in the space of the fourth dimension.

The extraordinary works taking place through handkerchiefs are also the works transcending space and time. Even with the passage of time, as long as the owner of the handkerchief is proper in the sight of God, the power contained in it does not disappear. Therefore, a handkerchief which is prayed on is very precious, for it can open the space of the fourth dimension anywhere.
But if one uses the handkerchief in an ungodly manner without any faith, there won't be any work of God. It's not just the one who is praying with the handkerchief but also the one who is prayed on who is supposed to be in accordance with justice. He has to believe that the handkerchief contains the power of God without any doubt.

In the spiritual realm, all things are done exactly and precisely according to justice. Thus, the faith of the person who is praying and that of the person who is being prayed on is measured precisely and the work of God will be manifested accordingly.

4. Utilizing Spiritual Space

Joshua 10:13 says, *"...And the sun stopped in the middle of the sky and did not hasten to go down for about a whole day."* This happened when Joshua had a battle against the Amorites while conquering the Canaan Land. How can the time stop for about a day in the first heaven?

A day is a period of time for the Earth to rotate once upon its axis. Therefore, for the time to stop, the Earth's rotation has to stop. But if the Earth's rotation stops, it will have a catastrophic effect not only on the Earth itself, but also many other celestial bodies. So, how could the time stop for almost a day?

It was made possible because not just the Earth but everything in the first heaven was in the flow of time of the spiritual realm. The flow of time in the second heaven is faster than that of the first heaven, and the flow of time in the third heaven is faster than that of the second heaven. But the flow of time in the fourth heaven can be either faster or slower than that of other heavens. In other words, the flow of time in the fourth heaven can vary freely according to God's intentions, as He harbors it in His heart. He can extend, shorten, or stop the flow of time itself.

In the case of Joshua, the whole first heaven was covered by the space of the fourth heaven, and time was extended as needed. In the Bible, we can see another account where one was on a shortened time flow. It was the case when Elijah ran faster than the chariot of the king in 1 Kings chapter 18.

The shortened time flow is the opposite of extended time flow. Elijah was just running at his own speed, but because he was on the shortened time flow he could run faster than the king's chariot. The works of creation, reviving the dead, and works that transcend time and space are done on the time flow that has stopped. That is why in physical world the particular work is done immediately upon the command or by harboring it in heart.

Let us look into what was like 'teleportation' of Philip, in Acts chapter 8. He was guided by the Holy Spirit to meet the Ethiopian eunuch at the road that descends from Jerusalem to Gaza. Philip preached the gospel of Jesus Christ and baptized him with water. Then, Philip suddenly appeared in a city called Azotus. It was kind of 'teleportation'.

For this teleportation to take place, one has to pass through the spiritual passage that is formed by the space of the fourth dimension, which has the characters of the fourth heaven. In this passage the flow of time is at a halt, and that is why a man can move a distance instantaneously.

If we can utilize this spiritual passage, we can even control the weather conditions. For example, suppose there are two places where people suffer from drought and flood respectively. If the rain of the flooding location can be sent to the place where they have drought, the problem of both places can be resolved. Even the typhoons or hurricanes are moved through spiritual passages to a place that is not inhabited, and it won't cause any problem. If we utilize the spiritual space, we can control not just typhoons but also volcano eruptions and earthquakes. It is that we can cover the volcano or the origin of the quake with the spiritual space.

But all these things are possible only when it is proper according to the justice of God. For example, to stop a natural disaster that affects a whole nation, it is proper for leaders of the country to request prayer. Also, even if the spiritual space is formed, we cannot go against the justice of the first heaven completely. The effects of the spiritual space will be limited to an extent where the first heaven won't suffer chaos after the spiritual space is lifted. God governs all the heavens with His might, and He is God of love and justice.

(End)

The Author
Dr. Jaerock Lee

Dr. Jaerock Lee was born in Muan, Jeonnam Province, Republic of Korea, in 1943. While in his twenties, Dr. Lee suffered from a variety of incurable diseases for seven years and awaited death with no hope for recovery. However one day in the spring of 1974 he was led to a church by his sister and when he knelt down to pray, the living God immediately healed him of all his diseases.

From the moment he met the living God through that wonderful experience, Dr. Lee has loved God with all his heart and sincerity, and in 1978 he was called to be a servant of God. He prayed fervently with countless fasting prayers so that he could clearly understand the will of God, wholly accomplish it and obey the Word of God. In 1982, he founded Manmin Central Church in Seoul, Korea, and countless works of God, including miraculous healings, signs and wonders, have been taking place at his church ever since.

In 1986, Dr. Lee was ordained as a pastor at the Annual Assembly of Jesus' Sungkyul Church of Korea, and four years later in 1990, his sermons began to be broadcast in Australia, Russia, and the Philippines. Within a short time many more countries were being reached through the Far East Broadcasting Company, the Asia Broadcast Station, and the Washington Christian Radio System.

Three years later, in 1993, Manmin Central Church was selected as one of the "World's Top 50 Churches" by the *Christian World* magazine (US) and he received an Honorary Doctorate of Divinity from Christian Faith College, Florida, USA, and in 1996 he received his Ph. D. in Ministry from Kingsway Theological Seminary, Iowa, USA.

Since 1993, Dr. Lee has been spearheading world evangelization through many overseas crusades in Tanzania, Argentina, L.A., Baltimore City, Hawaii, and New York City of the USA, Uganda, Japan, Pakistan, Kenya, the Philippines, Honduras, India, Russia, Germany, Peru, Democratic Republic of the Congo, Israel and Estonia.

In 2002 he was acknowledged as a "worldwide revivalist" for his powerful ministries in various overseas crusades by major Christian newspapers in

Korea. In particular was his 'New York Crusade 2006' held in Madison Square Garden, the most famous arena in the world. The event was broadcast to 220 nations, and in his 'Israel United Crusade 2009', held at the International Convention Center (ICC) in Jerusalem he boldly proclaimed Jesus Christ is the Messiah and Savior.

His sermons are broadcast to 176 nations via satellites including GCN TV and he was listed as one of the 'Top 10 Most Influential Christian Leaders' of 2009 and 2010 by the popular Russian Christian magazine *In Victory* and news agency *Christian Telegraph* for his powerful TV broadcasting ministry and overseas church-pastoring ministry.

As of November of 2015, Manmin Central Church has a congregation of more than 120,000 members. There are 10,000 branch churches worldwide including 56 domestic branch churches, and more than 103 missionaries have been commissioned to 23 countries, including the United States, Russia, Germany, Canada, Japan, China, France, India, Kenya, and many more so far.

As of the date of this publishing, Dr. Lee has written 100 books, including bestsellers *Tasting Eternal Life before Death, My Life My Faith I & II, The Message of the Cross, The Measure of Faith, Heaven I & II, Hell, Awaken Israel!,* and *The Power of* God. His works have been translated into more than 76 languages.

His Christian columns appear on *The Hankook Ilbo, The JoongAng Daily, The Chosun Ilbo, The Dong-A Ilbo, The Munhwa Ilbo, The Seoul Shinmun, The Kyunghyang Shinmun, The Korea Economic Daily, The Korea Herald, The Shisa News,* and *The Christian Press.*

Dr. Lee is currently leader of many missionary organizations and associations. Positions include: Chairman, The United Holiness Church of Jesus Christ; President, Manmin World Mission; Permanent President, The World Christianity Revival Mission Association; Founder & Board Chairman, Global Christian Network (GCN); Founder & Board Chairman, World Christian Doctors Network (WCDN); and Founder & Board Chairman, Manmin International Seminary (MIS).

Other powerful books by the same author

Heaven I & II

A detailed sketch of the gorgeous living environment the heavenly citizens enjoy and beautiful description of different levels of heavenly kingdoms.

The Message of the Cross

A powerful awakening message for all the people who are spiritually asleep! In this book you will find the reason Jesus is the only Savior and the true love of God.

Hell

An earnest message to all mankind from God, who wishes not even one soul to fall into the depths of hell! You will discover the never-before-revealed account of the cruel reality of the Lower Grave and Hell.

My Life My Faith II

Dr. Jaerock Lee's autobiography provides the most fragrant spiritual aroma for the readers, through his life extracted from the love of God blossomed in midst of the dark waves, cold yoke and the deepest despair.

The Measure of Faith

What kind of a dwelling place, crown and reward are prepared for you in heaven? This book provides with wisdom and guidance for you to measure your faith and cultivate the best and most mature faith.

Spirit, Soul, and Body I & II

A guidebook that gives the reader spiritual understanding of spirit, soul, and body, and helps him find what kind of 'self' he has made so that he can gain the power to defeat darkness and become a person of spirit.

Awaken, Israel

Why has God kept His eyes on Israel from the beginning of the world to this day? What kind of His providence has been prepared for Israel in the last days, who await the Messiah?

Seven Churches

The letter to the seven churches of the Lord in the book of Revelation is for all the churches that have existed up until now. It is like a signpost for them and a summary of all the words of God in both Old and New Testaments.

Footsteps of the Lord I & II

An unraveled account of secrets about the beginning of time, the origin of Jesus, and God's providence and love for allowing His only begotten Son Passion and resurrection!

The Power of God

A must-read that serves as an essential guide by which one can possess true faith and experience the wondrous power of God

www.urimbooks.com

www.ingramcontent.com/pod-product-compliance
Lightning Source LLC
LaVergne TN
LVHW021820060526
838201LV00058B/3456